A LIFE MEASURED IN SESSIONS

SEX, FITNESS, AND SELF-DESTRUCTION

CRAIG MALTESE

CONTENTS

Maltese, Craig, *A Life Measured in Sessions: Sex, Fitness, and Self-Destruction*

Copyright © 2019 by Craig Maltese

Published by KWE Publishing: www.kwepub.com

ISBN (paperback): 978-1-950306-03-9 (ebook): 978-1-950306-04-6

Library of Congress Catalog Number: 2019938876

What doesn't kill you...Gives you a lot of unhealthy coping mechanisms and a sick sense of humor.

~Unknown Author

DEDICATION

I dedicate this book to my wife, Grace. To me, she is truly the best part of every day and my life. I cannot begin to describe how grateful I am to her. She has stood by me through so many terrible situations of my creation, one after the other; ones that have caused her great pain as a woman, a wife, and a person. Through the many years in which I exhibited daily evidence of an underdeveloped emotional intellect and deteriorating moral fiber, she continued to pick me up in every sense of the word, every single time, over and over again. She is the one single person ever in my life who has never given up on me. She is the FIRST and ONLY person in my life that I have truly loved. Every day, she gives me unwavering encouragement and support to do the things I want to do in my life. There is no way I would be writing this book, and quite possibly without exaggeration, may not be alive today if not for her.

ACKNOWLEDGMENTS

A heartfelt thank you to Briar Dougherty, without whom this book would not be. Thank you to KWE Publishing for believing in me and my story.

FOREWORD

Working with Craig has been an adventure in and of itself. His wit and personal and professional dilemmas have been amplified by how he views the world, and seeing how that unravels and twists through his days is unique. We came to work together to help refresh his professional branding and sharpen his EQ skills. Through our collaborative relationship and shared experience, having worked in the health and fitness world, we quickly found our styles worked well together — both of us thriving in the transparency of our expectations and raw communication from each other.

He challenges me in every way – to be a better coach, to be firm in my thoughts, beliefs, and boundaries, and to create a message that resonates with someone exposed to so much hardship in their life. Writing this book with him, hearing his stories, and being the one who had to pull those sometimes hurtful, profoundly vulnerable, and personal memories to the surface has humbled me not only as a writer or a coach but as a human being. Life gives us all opportunities, some horrible, and some amazing. It is in those chance encounters that we can take steps that define our future.

I'm proud to say that I've been able to be a part of this journey with Craig. I've seen inside those hidden doors of his past and brought to life a story that so many others have dealt with in this world, in their unique settings, navigating life with their character flaws and default programming. It reminds me to stay grounded and open, and not to lay judgment on others without understanding the finer details of who they really are. For that, I'm proud of this book that Craig has created and so selflessly shared with the world. I hope that those who read it or meet Craig along their path find freedom in his words, humor in his narrative, and healing in their own time, shape, and manner.

Briar Dougherty, Founder & CEO of Career Organic

PREFACE

Years before the publication of this book, a friend, who at the time was an aspiring screenwriter, encouraged me to write down the stories I was sharing with her daily. She ultimately connected me with one of her literary agent friends who expressed interest in my writing ideas. But alas, I didn't follow through, and years would go by as more and more stories were being unearthed and logged into my vault. Her words of encouragement continued to reverberate for the next several years. Then one day, I just followed the words, and began to write, and write, and write.

I've asked myself over and over again, why did I decide to finally document these events? I realized that I have been walking through life with these stories in my head that feel like a 50-pound weight vest. As I started releasing these stories from their vault, I began understanding the deeper meanings and reasons for my behaviors over my life. I saw how each of these people, relationships, and events in my life shaped who I am today, and how I view it from an incredibly different lens than I previously did. I can now sit as an adult and recount what had happened. This book has been a way for me to express myself, and give my mind the freedom it's been needing for decades.

I'm sure there are people out there who have experienced much more adversity and were exposed to much worse conditions than I. Yet, they did not take the path I did. I want to make clear, I blame no one for the difficulties in my life. I almost always chose the path of least resistance rather than the path that would have provided positive growth and understanding. I alone am responsible; I could have and should have made better decisions. But that was my route and I fully embrace it.

The late author Christopher Hitchens famously said, "Everyone has a book in them, but in most cases, that's exactly where it should stay." I thought about that quote a lot while going through this writing and publishing process. No one was more critical than I of this work. However, I have developed a genuine appreciation, connection, and deep sense of ownership to my story, and sincerely believe that it will resonate in some way, SOME WAY, to everyone.

I hope you enjoy reading my story.

INTRODUCTION

With addiction becoming a wide-spread vice around the world, our minds have trained most of us to think about alcohol and substance abuse when we hear the word 'addict'. Neither of these vices has ever been a problem in my life. However, through the ravage of living amid the narcissistic tendencies of my mother, I became a victim, in all sense of the word, to the world of sex at a very young age. I'm talking about raw, dominatrix, hooker, exotic dancer kinds of fulfillment. Sex for sport, to be precise.

My story catalogs the erratic, yet comical, journey of a man on the road to finding out about life, relationships, sex, and that ever-elusive emotional intelligence as I fall prey to the enticements of the fitness industry.

This book recalls the calamity that became my life, with fitness as the catalyst for a tumultuous growth trajectory. As a socially awkward, uncomfortable teenager, I was looking for an escape from the campus of cookie-cutter, prefab students engrossed in study, socialization, and status. Stumbling upon a fitness facility far away from campus, I applied for a job and gained employment, thus commencing a path of reckless abandonment, deeply immersed within the seductions and intrigue of the fitness industry.

The story follows on my trek through mismatched relationships, a love-hate dynamic between my identity and how those around me actually perceived me, and how I always gravitated to the wrong crowd. Throughout the book, you will see my desire to grow, but not for the typical, conventionally aspiring reasons. As I reflect on growing up with my narcissistic mother, her sexual proclivity, and her lack of emotional sustenance lending to these inclinations, I'm reminded of how each decision she made for herself ultimately shaped my path. This dark and turbulent journey follows the unique point of view of a boy pushed into growing up too fast. Comedy was always lurking in the corners. It wasn't until much later that I grasped that fitness was not my calling.

Even though I have experienced success and periods of fulfillment in roles as owner, managing director, vice president, author, and podcast contributor across the fitness industry, given my upbringing, it's hard to reconcile I have held normalcy in my grasp. Each situation, moment, and relationship brought me closer and closer to my downfall. My hope in sharing these stories is that I put the word 'normal' on its edge, that I shine a light on the damage that parents can impose on their kids, and that the abnormal and atypical can survive in the world right alongside everyone else. While this is not the path I probably would have chosen initially, as if we have a choice, I came out of the craziness and landed on my feet. I am finally ready to tell my story and embrace humor as an asset in my arsenal of talents.

SESSION 1: MOMMY DEAREST

After a half-day at school, I come home early and meander lazily upstairs. As I walk halfway up, I peer right into her bedroom at eye-level.

Mommy's bedroom door is wide open. On the bed, I see her there, lying naked with a man. Grunting and breathing heavily, the man is coated with sweat.

Suddenly, they both turn to face me in the doorway. While the strange man sits up quickly, my mom covers her chest with a sheet, just like they do in soap operas.

Angrily she yells, "What are you doing home? Why aren't you in school?"

I freeze. There is no right answer; my mom does not want me home, no matter what the reason.

The man she is with is Rafael, a middle-aged, thin, bald man. After he leaves, my mother yells at my sister and me. "Damnit you two, Rafael asked me to move to San Francisco with him. But I told him no. I can't move anywhere because of you!"

She says this accusingly to my sister and me as if we have chosen to be born to spite her from having the carefree life she wants. I intrude on her life in every way – physically, emotionally, romantically, sexually, and on her aspirations.

I WAS a child at age 30 and a man when I was 10. Balancing the kid-man thing throughout my life lead me to a life of self-loathing and questioning my very existence in this world. Around the time I was entering the sixth grade, my parents finally stopped pretending to make things work. As long as it had taken them to reach this decision, there was no hesitation on my Dad's part to vacate the premises in an extraordinarily fastidious fashion. His vast arms reached out to my younger sister and me. "I won't be far, okay?" he whispered in our ears. His eyes seemed distant, caught in thought and not necessarily in the same moment as we embraced him, holding him tight. He slowly pried my hands from the top of his shoulders. The engine sputtered as he turned the key in the ignition. The tires crunched loudly on the small loose gravel and pebbles on the driveway. As he backed down, out of our driveway, I sat there in a state of disbelief, slumped over on the low stone wall that wrapped around the bottom of the hill. My shoulders were weighed by emotion as warm tears ran down my hot cheeks.

When the next Friday arrived, I sprinted off the bus and dusted off the most level spot along the wall, using the bottom of my t-shirt as a rag. I sat there, longing for him to drive up, like he had been on a work trip for the week, and would be returning the next weekend. I could hear my mom's voice echoing down the driveway from the top of the hill, "Craig, get your ass back up here. Dinner is ready." Unfortunately, I would grow very fond of this wall, as the concrete around its stone withered from the elements. Every weekend for the next several months, I sat there, hoping against all the odds that he would come back to visit us.

When that moment would happen, I vividly remember the sight of his car going ever so slowly around the turn that led to our driveway. If you didn't go slowly, you had the possibility of hitting whoever was at the bottom. Luckily for us, my father was not my mother and valued our well-being. Although for a while in our lives, he could not contribute toward our growth. We were faced with managing only one narcissistic parent, a task at which my sister and I both failed miserably. My dad stepped out of his brown and blue station wagon, his body moved slowly, and his shoulders heavy, an odd pose for him. With his muscular physique, chiseled jawline, and thick stature, he usually looked like a replica of John Gotti, but today, he looked worn, as if unsure of his authority as he stepped foot back on his old property.

"Daddy, is everything okay?" my sister asked. Her question caught him by surprise, and he shifted his weight, forcing a smile. "Of course, let's get going," he replied.

Our first stop was to the Sunset Diner in Green Brook. We walked in, my sister running up ahead and me right on her tail, with my Dad sulkily bringing up the rear. We were pulling out chairs to table when we heard our dad say, "In the corner," as he pointed over to a booth along the back of the dining area. We were the only ones sitting in that area.

The waitress rolled her eyes as she came to serve us, her mouth smacking up and down on some bubble gum, "What can I getcha?" she asked. My sister quickly looked down at the menu to avert the waitress's gaze, and so my dad began his order, with me going last. "I'll have a pizza burger deluxe," I said with a bit of extra enthusiasm. My mouth was practically watering, waiting for something that tasted better than the grilled cheese sandwiches we had been living off of for the prior 3 weeks. Our mom had declared, "I am not cooking every night for you kids! You either eat this grilled cheese or go to bed hungry." The small brown-haired waitress came back to our table with ice water in large plastic red cups. Our food arrived shortly after. The rest of our dinner was quiet until we made our way to the exit of the diner. "Thank you, Daddy," we both said in unison. "You don't have to thank me, you're my kids," he said endearingly, slightly blushing from the awkwardness of being thanked for something he took as a part of his role as our dad.

It had become a tradition to frequent Bowcraft Amusement Park, and we would go straight to the arcade after a round of mini-golf. We loved spending that last hour enjoying each other's smiles and laughter. The freedom was tangible, with no silly conversation or awkward pauses for the three of us. As we piled back into the car, my dad asked, "You guys still up for some ice cream tonight?" "Yes!" we both shouted emphatically. We drove up to the Howard Johnson on Route 22. Our eyes bulged as we looked at all the flavors of ice cream to choose from. I selected a Mint Chocolate Chip Hot Fudge Sundae, served chilled in a traditional tall ice-cream glass. These nights were ones to remember, and I still cherish the look on my dad's face, seeing that he could make my sister and me so happy, with the simple pleasures in life.

My sister started to sniffle in the back seat as the station wagon drove up the driveway. "Daddy, we miss you," she sobbed as she hugged him goodbye. His face was again unhinged, his eyes scanning the front door of the house as if he was preparing for something to jump out and scare us all. My mind was racing, and then the light bulb went off in my head. I understood why his face was so twisted, and his eyebrows looked furrowed. He was trying to avoid my mother. If he had only known the full onslaught of her resentment and defamation she was reaping through her words to us behind the comfort of her acutely designed and constructed sanctuary. She had no interest in preserving our love or attention in him anymore. She blamed him for every problem we encountered, had us checking the mailbox for his child support checks, and refused to encourage us to reach out to him. She had removed any photos in the house that included him in them. She had erased his memory from her mind and our home. Things changed rapidly; my sister and I were stuck in the twister that was our new life.

My mother had me quite late in her life. I was the third of four children. My two brothers were 12 and 14 years older than me, respectively, and my sister was 2 years younger. Throughout my childhood, I remember asking my mom why I was born so much later than my brothers were. Her reply was always, "Because your father wouldn't leave me alone." I didn't get it then; I do now.

Quicker than a hooker grabs cash off of a nightstand, things turned from bad to worse for my sister and me. My two older brothers had already moved out and had started their adult lives. My mom, now in her prime years, was ready to relive her youth, and to forget all about having children. The days and years to come would shape my life forever.

To make money, and not to depend on my father to have a job or send us any support, my mom decided to convert our humble home into a boarding house. If you are imagining the scene from the movie "Forest Gump" where his mom rented out rooms to the likes of Elvis Presley, you are not even close to picturing my reality. My mother felt empowered by receiving this rental income. It wasn't for her children, our well-being, or our comfort of living; it was in pursuit of financial independence, and that added to her confidence in navigating the inner workings of people in her life. She quickly converted our four bedrooms to make room for more boarders. As the number of tenants grew, my sister and I found ourselves bunking with mom.

People came and went from our house. Some stayed for a week, but others stayed longer. We had lots of contract workers due to the new AT&T plant being located nearby, and this kept the pipeline of paying occupants coming and going seamlessly. Days grew interesting. I looked around my house as if on a movie set. I imagined the strange men were random actors roaming about trying to be in good graces with my mother. As summer took full bloom, our house reeked of humidity, body odor, and on most days, burnt toast. The one window air conditioning unit in the house was in my mother's room. When the door was left open, we would see a congregation of renters outside the room, soaking up the cold air when they could. I was thankful at that time to be stuck in my mom's bedroom, as my sweaty body feeling the reprieve of cold air at night made up for the cramped quarters. My sister kept to herself quite a bit during these times, not wanting to catch the eye of any of the strangers walking around our small hallways. I didn't mind the company; however, sharing every inch of our house with these new people took a lot of adjustment. Our days ended quicker as our mom would shuffle us to our shared bedroom. My sister and I, in our makeshift beds on the floor with whatever clean sheets were availably strewn about them, tried to pretend to each other, and to our mom, that everything was normal. "Goodnight Mommy. I love you," both my sister and I would say sheepishly before laying down in our bed. "Just go to sleep both of you," she would answer most nights. It was rare, but cherished when she would reply, "Me too."

One morning I came into the kitchen. My mom sat at the kitchen table with her brown hair pinned neatly back, her blue slippers and matching bathrobe on, and a cup of coffee in her left hand. She was writing on a piece of paper that lay next to an open newspaper. "Mommy, what are you doing?" I asked. "None of your beeswax, Craig," she replied with a huff. "Get yourself some break-fast and go outside and play," she demanded firmly. It was days later I realized what she had been doing. It was her first attempt at personal ads in the local newspaper.

It was the early 1980's, back in the days of newspapers and land-line phones, when people would use personal ads for all kinds of things: finding jobs, locating lost pets, and in Mom's case, trolling for companionship. Personal ads were like a full-scale Tinder, without the app, and minus any of the bells and whistles. Black ink on paper, grassroots, personal marketing in its fullest form. Having a proactive mother such as mine, she formulated her pitch and forced my sister and me to rehearse our new life story. We were firmly instructed not to mention our older brothers, and she made a concerted effort to remove all pictures of the family from the house to effectively corroborate her story. My sister and I were required to reinforce her façade of being roughly 15 years younger than she was, and we didn't dare test this boundary.

At this point, before the influx of men, my sister and I were still mourning the loss of not having an outlet with Dad. It was hard to have our mom agree to call him or find the time when he would be available. Not seeing him as he drifted in and out of different homes and struggled to find career success in the construction business was difficult for us. Instead of responsible parenting, our house had become a melting pot of sketchy people, hermits, and occasionally, we were fortunate to have renters who were sweet and showed us compassion, playing ball in the front yard or watching movies with us.

Our brothers would come back to visit; both of them were married, and had to find convenient times to visit. They would pick us up to get us out of the house. I remember the joy I had when they would arrive. Tony, my eldest brother, always drove around the house to park in the back driveway, and as he rounded the corner and his Doo Wop music permeated the house, it was our call to action... our brother is here!!!! His white t-shirt was tucked neatly into his jeans and black leather jacket draped over the front seat of his red 1976 Pontiac Grand Prix. "Tony!" we would yell. "Hey, you two, ready to go?" he would say as he stepped out of the car to give us hugs. My mom would always stay inside, on occasion, giving a wave from the front kitchen window if she waited long enough for him to see her. Both of my brothers were in their mid-twenties now. They were thoughtful about choosing activities we would want to do; toss a football, go to a museum, or do something that would allow us some fun and time to bond. I still don't know to this day if they fully understood what was happening, and if they did, I'm not sure they would have been able to do anything about it, anyway. The repercussions of our mother's 'her- first' approach to parenting would wreak its havoc in their adult lives as well.

Months flew by, and leaves were now falling to the ground. They had changed from vibrant reds, oranges, and yellows to pale brown. They scattered across the yard and driveway. Mom piled us into the car and said, "We are going to visit some friends." When we got to the house, however, I didn't recognize it. I asked, "Who are we visiting?" All my mom could muster up was, "It's a friend; that's all you need to know."

And there we were, my sister and me, stuck in some stranger's house, as my mom took off in the car for the weekend. We sat in the living room, awkwardly for the first hour. The man and woman with whom she dropped us off showed us little hospitality. We ate a microwaved meal of meatloaf, mashed potatoes, gravy, and corn. There weren't a lot of choices back then, but we ate quietly as the couple watched TV, and waited for our mom to return. We were shuffled into a small room after dinner, which meant we were sleeping there. My sister and I shared a small bed, and both of us tried hard to go straight to sleep. Mom would return the next day to pick us up, without explanation. And so began the next year of our life.

As she walked in the kitchen, I knew just what to do. I'd been practicing replaying the scene in my head all day at school. As she was trying to ignore me studiously, I grabbed a glass from the cabinet. I got a carton of milk out of the fridge. My mom's hands were folded across her blue terrycloth robe. Pouring a half-inch into a glass, I swirled it around, took a swig like it were a shot of scotch, and put the glass down abruptly on the table. I looked at my Mom, trying to catch her eye, and said, "Hell of a day."

While I was sure I said the line the same way I had heard it on the then-popular show "Dallas" the night before, my Mom replied, "What is the matter with you? Just drink your milk or get the hell out of the kitchen."

Sheepishly, I said, "You know..." I stopped, watching the corners of her mouth as she cracked a small smile.

She walked away abruptly. I know I had made her smile. It was our small way of connecting, through humor. I made a conscious effort to behave more like I thought a man would. From my perspective, I thought she enjoyed me more that way. Secretly I was hoping she would resent me less if I didn't appear or act so young.

SHE WAS SOON in full pursuit of men, time alone, and was feeling like a free woman. Both of my older brothers were ushered in as babysitters when she couldn't find a friend or other alternate residence for us to stay during her weekend escapades.

Winter was in full effect, and if you know New Jersey in the winter, it's dark, cold, and relentless. Unless you have a parent willing to buy you appropriate clothing, you're stuck inside.

My mom had started taking me to the grocery store with her to 'help'. As we walked up and down the aisles, she practiced her best beauty-pageant smile with her male onlookers. One night, I caught her glance, and we locked eyes; they were angered and annoyed, her eyebrows high in the air. She quickly told me, "go check out the produce aisle, and I'll meet you there," as she walked away from me. As I obeyed, I heard a man's voice, "Hey, doll, looking good." He said to my mom. "Oh Roy, stop that, you'll make me blush," she replied with a flirtatious tone and light giggle. Her smile was real, and I started to understand a bit more about what was happening to my mom.

My mother was calling in several personal ads into the local newspaper weekly by now. Within weeks, men began to show up at our house to 'date' my mother. It appeared to be an exciting time for her. She was fulfilling her missed years of being in her late teens or early twenties again. She was enjoying both the freedom of feeling young and having the maturity to know precisely what she wanted, SEX! She must have thought it was now her time, and she was entitled to do whatever she wanted. And SHE DID! As each man would enter her life, my mother seemed calmer and happier in her body and her life. She would eventually clear out a room for my sister and me to sleep in so that we wouldn't be in the way in her bedroom.

As a stunning clone of Sharon Angela, who played Rosalie Aprile in "The Sopranos", my mom, both in looks and demeanor, was able to captivate men by the dozens. Winning their wallets, their love, their attention, and most of all their physical desire, all directed solely at her, consumed her. This new lifestyle became her new drug, her addiction, and her attempt to fill a missing piece of her soul with an insatiable appetite.

As her dates turned into relationships, she began realizing how much of a burden my sister and I were. We quickly became the primary obstacle standing in the way of pursuing her total fulfillment, if you will. During this period, my mom did what she could to keep it all going. However, it was clear that her priority was no longer my sister and me, but rather these men and her dalliances. In the beginning, she would invite them over and tell us to go upstairs and stay in our room. Of course, we didn't; there was no TV, phone, or anything else that might have kept us busy. We would hang out at the top of the landing in stealth mode. Most of the time, we tried to be inconspicuous. It was not a fun experience to be caught making noise or disrupting date nights for her.

After several dates, my sister became less interested and much better at finding something to do than I was. My curiosity about what was going on downstairs, and what I would eventually see, had a lasting effect on my life, and would ultimately become the most significant challenge I would face.

I began to get more and more curious about my mom's activities, as her dating schedule became quite busy. I began to see her patterns. Whenever she started prepping a nice dinner and dessert, I always knew we would be expecting a 'gentleman caller'. My mom never gave us sweets or delicacies, so my sister and I always looked forward to any chance to sneak some leftovers from the table. My sister and I would prepare for the date ahead of time, as we weren't allowed downstairs during her rendezvous. We would grab whatever food we could from the kitchen and any belongings we wanted from downstairs before the man would arrive, as my mom had become so preoccupied that she was no longer concerned with our meal schedule. The kitchen was right next to the dining room, so if we were hungry, we had to wait until whatever time we could safely access the kitchen. This time was most commonly after they had settled down in the living room over cocktails, or after the snuggling and giggling started.

Eventually, like clockwork, my mom and her date would retire to her bedroom, or in some cases, when my mom considered our virgin ears, they would disappear to a spare bedroom downstairs, depending on our current vacancy of renters. I always knew when that happened as the house became void of her fake laughter and the clinking of glasses.

This time of the evening became a game for me. One night, I sought out the action and peered through the open space between the old latch handle of the wooden door. I watched everything. Every movement, every piece of clothing I could see coming off, his white t-shirt, her stockings, his belt, her dress, and it continued until no more clothing remained. I held my ear to the open space, listening intently to the noises from within the walls of the room. Their breathing sped up, there were slight moans, and he would occasionally let out words of satisfaction. It has taken years to connect the dotted line to the images imprinted into my mind at that age, and the shadow that would follow me into my adulthood.

I watched and watched, and watched — different man, a different meal, the same result each date.

Soon, she became more brazen. That was the day I came home and saw her with Rafael. She made it very clear that we were ruining it for her.

That was the message from my mom for the next year. How all these men loved her and wanted to whisk her away, but we were the reason she couldn't go. I felt unwanted and very lost. My mother became increasingly angry, resentful, and impatient with us, her two children who couldn't take care of themselves.

As time passed, the dysfunction became a part of everyday life. My dad was still drifting in and out of our lives. I never realized how angry she was until one day in November, when I was 12 years old. I was playing with leaves in our yard and running around. It was something I loved to do, could do alone, and did every fall season. As I was playing around one of the huge trees in our front yard, I slipped and landed headfirst into the massive tree trunk. The hard, sharp bark opened a deep cut on the top of my head. As I touched my head, I felt the warmth of blood streaming steadily down my face. I collected myself and ran inside, yelling out to my mom, who was upstairs in her bedroom applying nail polish. She rushed downstairs to hear me sobbing and recounting what had happened. "Mommy, I hit my head on the tree. It hurts, Mommy, it hurts." She grabbed my head to find the cut and became apoplectic. Grabbing my shoulders, she began to shake me and yell, "Why? Why? What's the matter with you? I can't take it anymore!!!"

She continued to throttle me as her anger reached its peak, at which point she began to slap my face and head. I did my best to block the barrage, but her rage and hand speed were no match for my tiny frame and the fear that had frozen me in place. I just stopped and hoped she would let up. She did and eventually took me to get stitches.

Sitting at the doctor's office, she could barely make eye contact with me. She was furious. I sat there with my head burning as they poured antiseptic into the wound before stitching it up. I kept looking over when I could to see her. She sat there in the chair in the corner of the room, and I could tell that she had honestly had about enough with being the sole caretaker of her children.

I felt like she loved me. However, it was a strange love, one that came with contingencies and lots of rules. At that point in her life, she didn't like being a mom anymore. That's what I told myself and still do to this day, though she died many years ago. She was over it and wanted to be free. As an adult, I can now understand her narcissistic ways; my sister and I were an extension of her. We were in her way, and she felt trapped. She was capable of doing anything to anyone, at any time, in any way she could, to attain her freedom, no matter who it hurt. She felt entitled to this life of freedom, sex, romance, travel, and leisure, and devoted the rest of her life chasing it.

Growing up, my mother always spoke to me like an adult, never like a child. I guess it was due in part to her apparent lack of patience for kids at that time. I'm still on the fence as to whether motherhood was innate or if her narcissism consumed those genes.

There was a big-time gap between us, compounded by the fact that my parents married very young, and then had four kids separated by 16 years.

My mom had a good run for her money when it came to dating and a good pick of gentleman callers from which to choose. During this time, she weighed her options, and her moods shifted on a steady yet turbulent schedule like the tide. As the weather changed again, the warmth was in the air, and the sun was out longer, I took advantage of this change in scenery. One night I took a walk around my yard. "This is a stickup!" I yelled. "Bang Bang!" I shouted as I pointed a stick I had found in the yard toward my nemesis, the old tree which had sliced open my head. I got a sense of release from playing out scenes I had watched in movies or on TV. I would fall deep within the fantasy about the people I wanted to be like and the things I wanted to do.

Reflecting on those dear memories, I realize it was an escape, and gave me something happy and positive on which to focus. Aside from visits from my brothers, I didn't have many things to look forward to, so these moments were an integral part of keeping me sane as a child. I was shaken back into reality every time I returned to Mom's house after a visit, and I would have to accept my fate all over again.

My mom's flings were now evolving into longer relationships. We went out one morning in the car. My mom was wearing a burgundy dress, with fancy new shoes. The only reason I knew they were new was that as we got into the car, she commented, "Don't either of you step on my new shoes. I want them looking amazing for our friend!" We arrived at the local restaurant, and my mom rushed ahead of us to embrace this tall, dark-haired man. His shirt opened wide, buttoned halfway up, showcasing a full chest of hair, and three gold chains dangling from his neck. I remember he had piercing blue eyes, and those eyes spent the entire breakfast gazing intently at my mother. She giggled and laughed as the man acted like he knew my sister and me. She was acting like we were a big family and this strange man was a part of it. It was like some superhero 'surrogate dad for a day' was bestowed upon these poor souls.

After helping one man move in so he could embark on his prize with more frequency, their relationship would last for a few months before I was moving him back out, and so on. One day, a different man appeared. This man came into our house with a new stance. He had a similar entitlement as my mom, to have what he wanted and when he wanted it. Enter Bernie, exit all boarders.

Bernie was a smart man, with square black glasses that framed his brown eyes and added an air of intellect. He was an engineer by trade. He met my mom the same way all of the other drifters had. Bernie had two sons from his previous marriage who were much older than my sister and me, and as time passed, we would have minimal contact with them.

I arrived at the trailer park to help him move. Collecting his boxes from the dirtied trailer, I coughed continuously from handling the items in his smoke-filled room that traveled with us the entire car ride back to my house. Upon his arrival, the air in our home filled with a new blanket of smoke, permeating the walls and furniture with the potent aroma of Pall Mall cigarettes. I had briefly thought he had done us a favor by getting rid of the boarders, assuming this evacuation would have normalized our home, but I was wrong yet again. He was a packrat. He filled our once spacious and neat home with boxes of junk, in which he would spend hours just sifting through and smoking. That seemed to be his hobby. At least it was when he wasn't hovering over my mother.

I would go on long walks and spend hours in my room to escape and to stay safe from exploding at my mom or Bernie. My days had become mundane, listening to rants of "Craig, get your room cleaned up!" and "Craig, why haven't you taken out the garbage yet? Get moving!" The room that I was now in happened to be my brother Dino's old room. There were lots of trinkets and bags left behind by a boarder who had been staying in that room. One day, while playing in the closet, I came upon a dark brown leather duffle bag. Inside that bag was a large stack of "Playboy" and "Penthouse" magazines. I began to read through them. Well, I did not necessarily read them, but I did look at them every single day.

I often reimagine those moments now as an adult; I was quite young and did not have much formal or informal sex education, outside of watching through the keyhole of my mother's bedroom. These magazines and visual images, combined with my mother's live events in the house, began to create a compelling and dysfunctional perspective of sex and intimacy. Nevertheless, it consumed my attention, and I began to act more like the adult my mom always pretended she was speaking to, and less like the child I should have been.

Bernie and I wouldn't become friends. We would be the point of contention in the house that smothered happiness, produced scared smiles, and brought toxicity to every crack in the old wooden floors. He believed in the oppressive hand policy. If you didn't get in line, there were physical consequences. I don't think he was an evil man exactly. I think he didn't know any better and thought he was giving us what he was supposed to give. I like to believe that; the alternative is much sadder and one that hurts. I was in trouble much more often than my sister for any number of reasons: being late, not finishing chores, or mouthing off. Claudine fell in line, avoiding Bernie's wrath. "Yes sir," she would answer Bernie as he demanded a beer from the fridge. I did not take so kindly to directions; therefore, I found the brunt of Bernie's anger quite often.

As a young teen, I was more than challenging. I was angry, filled with resentment, and so awkward with life and people that there was nowhere to go. I would spend hours and hours outside. I knew that if I could wait out Bernie, he'd call in for a nightcap and fall asleep.

My mother remained so negligent and oblivious that she married this abuser. With the new title of husband, Bernie took a more significant step up his pedestal, and the demands and consequences on us were now more elaborate. My brothers played a vital role in helping me through these times. They would each take turns coming and getting me, or both my sister and me, on week-ends to get out of the house. Every time I was dropped off at home, I would cry. I would watch as their car would pull away down the driveway, and the misery would seep back into me like a dark cloak or a mist that rolls in off of the water in a Jason Voorhees horror film. In the way that you can feel your skin start to stand up, waiting for the villain to jump out and wreak his havoc upon your body, your emotions, and evoke your deepest fears, I felt the same dread.

During this time, my brother Tony took heart to my situation and helped revitalize the gym he had used during his college years. He set up an exercise circuit for me in the basement, filling the tiny wall space with giant posters of Arnold Schwarzenegger and Rocky. One afternoon he had come over to 'babysit' for my mom. My sister lay upstairs in our mother's room and watched TV. We went down-stairs, leaving Claudine by herself. Tony showed me how to use the weights he had set up and how to create a workout. I felt amazing. It was like a fire had awoken inside me. My muscles responded to every movement, and the release that I needed for so long was there. I watched as I did an arm curl with a ten-pound weight. My veins pulsed, and my bicep grew in size. I felt powerful.

Tony shared with me the trope, 'No pain, no gain'. But more importantly, he looked around the basement and said, "This is yours now, Knoopy," his nickname for me. My nook, my 'man space,' was tucked neatly next to the washing machine. My mom would come down into the basement to do laundry, staring at me like I had eight arms. I quickly learned what she was thinking, as she rarely kept her thoughts to herself. "Craig, you look silly trying so hard," she would say. I had created a habit, though, and her comments would only further fuel my intent.

I found a pair of heather grey sweatpants and cut them to fit me. I went outside to go on a run throughout the neighborhood, pumping my fists like Rocky Balboa. The thrill I got from my work-outs lit my passion further, and I made it a routine to run after school every day. Exercise became a part of my escape, and a place where I could feel normal, whatever that meant to me then. I didn't know that this serenity would be something I would crave more than anything for a very long time.

One day while my mother was making coffee, I walked into the kitchen to pour myself a cup of orange juice. As I poured the remainder of the carton into my cup, my mother came over to me. "You know Craig, I ran into a neighbor in the grocery store, and she was seriously asking me if you had some type of mental development issue, running around the neighborhood waving to everyone. What is wrong with you?" she asked. I just shrugged my shoulders and said, "I dunno," and walked out of the kitchen, knowing full well that I had been running around the neighborhood waving to everyone, reenacting Sylvester Stallone's scene in the "Rocky II" training montage as he ran through the streets of Philadelphia.

Every Saturday evening during the autumn season, Bernie and my mother would go out to dinner. The rule was to rake up and pile all the leaves in the yard before they returned. I hated this chore. I didn't enjoy manual labor, and I certainly didn't feel it necessary to do anything that would remotely help out Bernie. So, I would gather the leaves up in small piles and then run and jump into them. I got such enjoyment out of making things a game. It was on one of these nights that I struck a chord with the old enforcer. Maybe it was too much drink left in him from dinner or just an excuse to do something to me because he disdained my very presence. We will never know. My mom and Bernie pulled up into the driveway and parked the car. He walked out from the driver's seat, took a mental picture of the leaf-ridden yard, and walked over to his shed. I remember my paralysis as I saw him walk briskly across the yard with a 2 x 4 piece of wood, about three feet long. He had been working on this piece of wood and had crafted a handle of sorts by thinning off one end so he could get a better grip. I can remember seeing the wood shavings on it, as he didn't sand it after the trim. For an older gentleman, he moved swiftly and accurately, and caught me across my backside, knocking me to my knees. He reared back up again and swung baseball style and caught me in my lower back for the second blow. I remember holding back my sounds as I fell forward toward the ground, too proud to admit defeat to this sleaze bag. Feeling the burn of embarrassment heat my face, I quickly ran to my room once the stun wore off.

I painfully walked into class the next day and was promptly sent to the nurse's office. After she examined me and saw the bruising that had already set in, it was apparent someone had struck me across my back with something multiple times. She turned to me, eyes wide, filled with anger and sadness all in the same moment and asked: "Who did this to you?" I lifted my arms to the sides in a gesture that said I didn't know. After a long back and forth in that manner, she asked if I'd like to speak with someone else about what had happened. I agreeably shook my head. My dad was the only person to whom I knew I could talk. I fought back the urge to cry and scream, and I tried to compose myself a bit as I stood there on the rotary phone. "I'm in the nurse's office, Daddy. They are making me tell them what happened. Bernie hit me with a piece of wood. I don't know what I should tell them. I'm scared; I don't want him to do it again if I tell on him." I stammered out. My dad was very calm and just listened.

My dad was always so hard to read. Sometimes he was amazingly patient, he wasn't a hothead, and didn't get angry easily, or at least he never showed it. His focus was primarily on wanting things to be better than they were. He called child services on Bernie. The next day, I was being interviewed at my middle school by a child welfare social worker. My brother Dino, now divorced with a child of his own, had moved in with my dad. After hearing the news of the abuse, he paid a visit to Bernie and let him know this would be the last time he laid a hand on me.

Later that week, my dad took me out to our favorite diner. I sat there, staring at him, his thick neck tense, and yet I noticed a calmness in his face. If you didn't know him personally, his physicality would have been intimidating. He looked like a strong and serious Italian man. His demeanor was anything but, however, as he was not menacing, nor did he have any sinister ulterior motives directed at anyone.

When Italian families immigrated to the United States, they either chose to continue to exert their strength, or to succumb to the pressures of assimilation. My dad had adopted the ideals of a pacifist, and as he sat across from me, I had only one thought on my mind. I asked, "Can I come live with you?" I can still see his face as he answered, "Yes." There was no hesitation, no waver in his voice. I felt the rush of relief fill my body. I had won the lottery and was finally moving out of that hellhole.

My sister would stay for a brief stint with my mom and Bernie as was her decision, and I moved out. My mom barely spoke to me as I left the house. Her posture was stiff, her hair was curled up in its mask of hair spray, and she looked ready to go out for a night on the town. She showed none of the remorse or the disheveled scene you might imagine would occur as a mother's young child packs his suitcases to leave. You could see the slight smile peeling over her face, knowing that she had one less burden. It must have been a relief in so many ways for her.

My new pad was a small, three-bedroom house that my dad and brother were sharing. I moved my gym equipment and the rest of my stuff. My dad had formed his own drywall construction company and landed a large development project in Lakewood, New Jersey. These were the best career years of his life. During this time, my view of my father was that he had an incredibly intense work ethic, that he was a 'take care of business' type of person, and that he was always pushing to improve. Today, looking back, I realize how much of a struggle each day was for him to keep it all going despite the many personal and professional setbacks he experienced. He was a loner, and loners love to be alone.

He found great solace in hopping into his truck each day; it was his refuge. He would find a local coffee shop and eat the same breakfast every day, a buttered roll and coffee, and sit in his truck while reading several newspapers cover to cover. He loved being at the job site and relished the ability to work alone. That was the only environment where a loner like him could have existed. There was some interaction on the job site; his crew would call him 'Gotti', and he played along.

My dad's reactions to events were often out of proportion to the situation. My brother Dino tells of a story when he and Tony were little kids. One day, Dad stopped the car. "Get me some soft serve chocolate ice cream," he said to Dino. He let Dino and Tony out to run across the street to get his cone and their own. When they returned to the car and told him they were out of chocolate ice cream, my father, clearly upset, exclaims, "JESUS CHRIST! How can they NOT have CHOCOLATE! They only sell two GODDAMN flavors!" He hit the steering wheel with a closed fist in frustration. Conversely, on another occasion, someone stole his car. He had a habit of leaving the keys in the ignition. He didn't react to that at all. As a result, I often modeled after him and became overly involved in the wrong things, explosive in my response, and then timid and passive for something needing much more emotion.

Once I got settled, my dad proposed sending my sister to a private Catholic boarding school. My mother jumped at the first mention of this suggestion. My sister dove into religion, finding sanctuary in the safety of the church and those around her. She attended school full-time and thus was spared the remainder of the Bernie regime before my mom split up with him eventually.

We created a routine, our new family unit. It was my second eldest brother Dino, Dad, me, and my sister Claudine, who would visit on the weekends. It was still dysfunctional, but it was far less stressful daily.

SESSION 2: SUMMER LOVIN'

I am eye-to-eye with my grandmother, which is strange because she is barely over 5 feet tall, and I usually tower a good 7 to 8 inches above her eyeline. She is furious.

My friend Ray and I return home way past our curfew. Knowing we are in trouble, we begin the mile walk back. When we are within about a hundred yards, we can make out two figures, one very small and one significantly larger. As we approach, it is clear that those two people are my grandmother and Ray's mother.

Ray's mom immediately grabs him and starts slapping him across the face like a rag doll. My grandmother, however, is silent and calm in front of me.

When she looks at me, it is so intense, like an X-ray blasting into my soul. She looks me dead in the eyes (again, how can this be? She's so much shorter than I am!) and quietly says, "I'm not going to tell your father about this. Don't ever do this again. If you do, you won't have to worry about your father; you'll have to worry about me. Do you understand?"

I say, "Yes, I do."

Even with her intense, squinty, raven-like eyes glaring straight at me, I know she cares about me. She is acting like she was my mother; the maternal role my actual mother rarely took.

Then there is a long pause. My grandmother says to me, "Are you hungry?"

I reply with an emphatic, "Yes!"

At this moment, I am saying yes to both her implicit questioning and exact words. Yes, Grandma, I understand you. Yes, I want to move on, too. And lastly, Yes, I want to eat.

Ray and his mother notice us and stand there with their jaws wide open. Here he is, a strong young man, and his mom is beating him like a rented mule. They can't understand why my grandma isn't slapping me senseless, too.

What they don't know, and my grandmother does, is there is already too much violence in my life. Bernie, my mother, everyone smacks down too hard. All kick and no hug. But what my grandmother does is just as stern without the overkill. It is just what I need.

I STRUGGLED to roll the window down in the back seat of the rented station wagon. After laboriously cranking the white handle on the door clockwise to get the pane of glass to creep open, the rush of warm air hit my face. Even in that heat, the air circulating throughout the car helped the beads of sweat on the underside of my legs cool me off.

It was the summer of my freshman year of high school; Dad rented a car and drove my sister and me to Florida. I remember the phone call he had with my grandmother before we left.

"Ma, yeah, I just need some time. I'm figuring it all out," he paused, nodding his head as if she could see him. And finally, he said, "Sure, that works. I can make it that weekend." He paused again, "I'll rent a car, it will be fine."

He was dropping me off with my grandmother for the entirety of summer vacation. During the next few summers, my dad would utilize my grandmother for a much-needed reprieve from my sister and me. Loading up the rental car with a cooler in the front seat, filled with M&Ms and treats for us, he ultimately kept us quiet and from asking "are we there yet?" a thousand times.

My grandmother, a traditional Italian woman, lived in Hallandale Beach, Florida. She stayed in a small retirement community called the Golden Bay Lodge. On one side was the ocean, and on the other was the bay. It was incredible! Located on South Ocean Drive, it was surrounded by large vacation condominiums and resort hotels.

I was 15 years old, full of energy, and looking forward to spending my days in the sunshine. I woke up the first morning to a fantastic breakfast of cinnamon toast, bacon, scrambled eggs, a choice of orange juice or milk, and a blueberry muffin. "Well, eat up," my grandmother lovingly said as she guided me by the small of my back toward the table. I had hesitated long enough, with eyes wide, and must have looked excited and bewildered. My grandmother's smile was ear-to-ear as she let out a small chuckle to herself. I ate everything she had laid out for me. I gulped down the orange juice, eggs, and bacon, and then hurried through the cinnamon toast and muffin, washing it down with a glass of milk. From that morning on, I lived in a little bubble, spending my days playing on the beach and being utterly spoiled by my grandmother.

I hadn't had a girlfriend up to this point and spent most of my time at a large condo community next door called the Hemispheres. Those days at the Hemispheres were some of the best of my life. It was one of the few periods of my childhood when I was able to be a kid. I felt loved and safe. My grandmother pulled me aside the first week I was there and said, "I just want you to have fun. I want you to spend time with your friends."

She doted on me and showed me off to her friends, running into them at the grocery store, or the mall. Every night we would get a spot in the living room, make a little bowl of ice cream, and watch "The Lawrence Welk Show", an old musical show that was family-friendly. I felt alive, like I was having the elusive summer vacation that the few friends I had back home always recounted to me. I wasn't seeing and hearing things that I shouldn't be seeing. What a breath of fresh air.

One of the first friends I made in Hallandale was Ray, who was visiting his grandmother a few units down from ours. As our friendship grew, we would frequently spend our days together. He would typically come to our condo door and knock for me to come out with him. "Your boyfriend is here," my grandmother would yell toward my bedroom. She was a spicy, humorous woman who took full enjoyment of my frustrations and embarrassments.

One night Ray and I went to South Ocean Drive ready for some fun. It was the '80's, and we had no security or supervision, and those Public Service Announcements saying, "It's 10 o'clock; do you know where your children are?" weren't out in full force yet. Our usual evening routine was to walk up to the Diplomat, which at the time was a very lively hotel, with unattended access from the beach about a mile up South Ocean Drive. Most nights were just that, a walk, a few laps around the pool, a leisurely stay in the lobby, a few minutes spent people watching, and returning back home in time for ice cream and TV with Grandma.

Freshman status in high school had rendered us too young to be in full swag with the females, yet we were hoping endlessly to get the company of just about any young, feminine company we could. Our luck changed one night when we met a couple of girls at the pool. They were cute, one blonde and one brunette.

I shimmied closer to them in the water. "Uhh, umm, I'm Craig," I said awkwardly. Ray quickly swam over, and with zeal, he practically shouted, "Yeah, and I'm Ray."

"Jessica," said the blonde, "and that's Amy," she continued, pointing to her brunette friend. We hung out by the pool and had a great time just being around actual girls. We found out that Amy was only there because she was forced to tag along with her mother, who was attending a local business convention. Jessica had been asked to join Amy to keep her company. After an hour of random stream of consciousness statements on the parts of Ray, me, and the girls, the time came where they were ready to leave.

"So do you guys want to come back to the room with us? My mom won't be back until really late tonight, and we have some alcohol," Amy said, facing me.

"Sure!" I exclaimed, before even glancing at Ray. Internally I was yelling for joy, until my nerves sullied the moment. What in the world were we doing? Were we going to get physical with some girls? My mind started contingency planning; the blonde was cute, but the brunette was kind of quiet, and that might be more fun. Then my nerves came back to me again, and I barely figured out how to dry myself off as I tripped out of the pool, my toe getting caught on the lip of the inground pool.

They weren't joking! They had a full bottle of rum and brought out a 2-liter bottle of soda. I offered to pour our first round of drinks. Jessica walked to the kitchenette in the hotel room and grabbed four glasses out of the cabinet. She looked at Ray and asked, "Could you go get ice from the machine down the hall?" He nodded his head "yes" without so much as a squeak from his mouth. He was back in no more than 15 seconds with ice. I poured a healthy portion of rum into each cup and then topped it with the soda. We all choked back the gag reflex at the strength of the alcohol, but each of us, eyeing one another, drank it down entirely and quickly. Jessica offered to pour our second drink, and as we loosened up, we each enjoyed laughter, jokes, and the exhilaration of each other's company.

Absorbed in the moment, Ray and I paid no attention to the clock, missing our reasonable curfew of 9:30 pm, and my TV and ice cream time with Grandma. We had completely forgotten about the family members who were expecting our safe return hours earlier. We could tell the girls were getting tired, and the excitement was winding down. I was so eager to get a kiss, I leaned in to say goodnight to Amy, but she threw her arms around my neck and hugged me instead.

"We had a great time!" she exclaimed as she walked over to Ray and hugged him. As the girls waved to us from their hotel room door, the elevator opened and we waved goodbye.

Whether or not we made a conscious choice not to call home in fear of being told to come back, or whether we just got lost in the festivities, I can't recall. I know it was about 11 pm when we landed in the lobby of the hotel and started our mile-long walk back home.

And as simple as our excursion had been, it was the last summer I hung out with Ray. I suppose his mom thought it was my influence that led him to make poor decisions. I can't argue that point. I seemed to always have difficulty following rules, a trait I inherited from my father.

The next summer, I met Dale, a very outgoing guy around my age, with a similar build and look to a younger version of the actor Paul Giamatti. Dale was fearless and would talk to anyone, especially girls. He had a real love for people and that was one of the most significant differences we would encounter in our friendship. I didn't share the same love or even 'like' of people, and still struggle with this as an adult. Dale's enthusiasm for people and connecting with them has stayed with me over the years. I was always puzzled by his intent and his lust for interaction for emotional connection. He enjoyed conversation and connecting in any way he could.

Unlike Dale, my connection was with the curves, the scents, and the innate appeal of the teenage female population with the hope of being physically, not emotionally, connected with them. I had developed a coping mechanism to survive my Mom and Bernie days, and hadn't learned to value conversation or company in the traditional ways most people do. Instead, I created excitement in interaction by thinking about the possibilities to connect bodily. It made conversation bearable with females at this age, with all of their ridiculous giggles and talk of hair, music, and parties.

Dale was a good influence on my social life that summer. He would encourage me to come out with other guys and meet up with big groups of people. I limited my interaction to a couple of times a week as I felt a bit depleted after these outings. "Craig, what do you think?" "Craig, tell me about where you are from," would be the initial questions from the group. With the spotlight on me, I couldn't maintain a sweet smile or face for long in those settings. I just avoided being the center of attention whenever it was possible.

I didn't know how dysfunctional I was, as I had not yet had a girlfriend, but there were signs. My sister came to visit for a week that summer, and we would frequent the mall together during these visits. One day we were walking from the food court, sodas in hand as we began our way to the arcade.

"I love Grandma's cooking!" my sister was saying. She had been missing out on all the spoiling from Grandma during the summertime and was enjoying her freedom. We both laughed and shook our heads "yes" to each other. We noticed a girl, short and curvy, with long dark hair draping down to the small of her back. She was walking by herself in front of us, and she seemed to be walking in the same direction. My sister tried talking again to me, but I was glazed over, intent on watching the hips of this beautiful girl sway back and forth in front of me. She noticed and walked right up to the girl.

"I'm Claudine! Me and my brother Craig are going to the arcade, how about you?" she said, as she turned her head to motion to me.

"I'm Lori," she spoke back without hesitation. My sister ushered me up to join them in the walk.

"Hi," I said. "Hi," Lori said back as her cheeks blushed.

We all entered the arcade and spent our entire time together. My sister separated off from the two of us after about 10 minutes. She was indeed a bona fide wing-woman for me that day.

Lori had sparked an interest in me. As we talked, we found out we were both living incredibly close to one another. I got her family's phone number. Landline phones were all we had at that time, so I made sure to get it! Before leaving the mall, we picked a time to have a phone call later that night. My grandmother, seeing me light up at the mention of this new 'friend' Lori, was more than eager to arrange a get-together with her at the condo. It's slightly ironic that I have my grandmother to thank for my first 'hands-on' experience with a girl! She had convinced my father it was okay to have her over.

It was another hot summer day when Lori arrived. I brought her up to meet my grandmother and told her, "We are going to go explore on the beach."

"Okay Craig, enjoy yourselves. Be back by 5 pm. Lori's father will be coming then to pick her up."

"I will, Grandma," I responded.

We decided to go out to the pool instead. I opened the gate and walked through, holding the heavy metal door for Lori. She walked quickly through, and we were standing extremely close. The tension between us made me sweat. My hands were clammy. She brushed past my shoulder and giggled. I knew right away she was flirting. She wanted me to make a move. ANY move.

I leaned in quickly and kissed her. Her lips were slippery, with some gloss on them. It was magical, and I don't use that word lightly. She kissed me back, and our bodies moved close together, with mine pressing into her chest and pushing her into the white-painted cinderblock wall behind her. We both stopped and breathed heavily. Smiling at each other, she reached down to hold my hand. I grasped it back and guided her to the building's maintenance room.

We spent uninterrupted hours groping each other in the building's maintenance room. Lori's skin was so soft. I ran my hand over her hips, up her back, and then down around her butt, memorizing each curve as we kissed. To give our lips a break and to get some much-needed drinks, we made a stop by the pool for a bit and went swimming while splashing each other flirtatiously. My eyes kept shifting to watch the time. I did not want to mess up by arriving back at my grandma's condo at a late hour. After we dried off from the pool and threw on a change of clothes from the soft canvas beach bag she had brought, we walked dreamy-eyed back to Grandma's condo.

About a week later, we coordinated another visit. I spent the day at her house this time, but with much more supervision. We did, however, find a way to evoke an encore performance nevertheless.

It was sloppy and messy and void of any real understanding, but it was fun!

Our attraction to one another made for a scene, however. A fuse was lit, and it was the last time we would see each other. Lori's parents confronted her after I left and called my grandma to let her know I was no longer allowed to visit.

"He is too physical with our daughter. We no longer will allow them to see one another," Lori's father said to my grandma. And that was the end of that. My grandma laughed as she told me what he had said, "Craig, you'll never make it past her father if you walk around staring at her rump."

Another girl would enter the fray; Andréa, pronounced 'On-Dray-Ah.' She was a petite, dark-haired girl from Long Island, New York. Her family was staying in the Hemispheres. We met at the pool, and I quickly stammered out some small talk. She had a black and white striped bikini. I was mesmerized with it and hoped she didn't notice.

"Would you like to hang out later today?" I asked with newfound confidence.

"Sure, where should we meet?" she asked.

"How about here around 7?" I suggested.

"Sounds great!" she said, as she dried off her legs with her pink towel.

I spent dinner thinking about her, her soft voice, and her striking brown eyes. Something pulled me to her, and I had a deep desire to spend time with her.

That afternoon, a few of the guys I met in the Hemispheres were planning a night out at a local dance club called Randolph's. But I secretly had my heart set on seeing Andréa and was afraid if I told them my intention, I would be teased and ridiculed. The evening came, and as I walked toward the pool deck to meet Andréa, I ran into the other guys while they were leaving. I neglected to share my alternate plan with them, and they swooped me up just as Andréa was getting to our meeting spot. I didn't open my mouth once! I didn't resist. I just turned longingly watching her face, her smile had faded, and she looked confused and angry.

I couldn't stop thinking about Andréa as we all drove off in the car. As soon as we arrived home from the club, I wrote her a letter and took it over to her apartment first thing the following morning. She and her family were packing up to head back to Long Island. She was surprised to see me, and it was like a scene out of a 1980's teen movie, music and all, only this was my movie.

Everyone in her family stopped what they were doing and watched as I handed her my note and walked away. I remember having all these feelings, both real and imaginary. I mean, I didn't even really know this girl, but when you are a teenager, it all seems so real and dramatic.

We would write to each other for a few months after summer ended. She wrote details about her new boyfriend. It stung knowing I had missed my opportunity. She was the first girl I had ever taken the time to be with emotionally. Well, I was as sensitive as you can be with no idea of what it meant to be a true friend. We both kept up periodic communications throughout the years. She eventually married a cop, began a career in education like both of her parents and settled down not far from where she grew up on Long Island. But that wasn't the end of the story. It would be 20 years before we met again and completed the circle.

SESSION 3: TEEN WOLF

Eighties dance music is blaring from the boombox, mounds of food are sitting uneaten, and no one is here to enjoy it. It is empty. As soon as Liz's sister Linda walks out onto the patio party room, she gives me serious side-eye. I can tell she is thinking, "Where the hell is everyone? What did Craig do?"

She is right, of course. I edited the invite list. Liz is so lovely and vibrant, and I want her all to myself. Now looking at the sad scene that should have been a joyous celebration, but is ruined because of me, I feel sick to my stomach. I keep sipping from my cup, long after there is nothing inside to sip, just to avoid eye contact. Sitting next to Liz, I realize I have gotten my way.

But at what cost? What impact will this have on us years later? Am I acting like my mom?

But, on this day, I don't even think about how it impacts Liz. I never do have a chance to say I'm sorry.

BACK IN NEW JERSEY, the school year proved challenging. Living once again with my dad and brother, I struggled to find my own space, my own identity, and my own life. I slowly developed friend-ships with some local kids around my age. We made a collective group of five, and it was the closest thing to friendship I had known other than my summers at my grandmother's place. Brad was my best friend in that group, and it was around this time we were all entering our pubescent peaks. We were sneaking pornography from one house to another, and were all trying to see who would get into the pants of the girls at school. I was one of the shyest of the group but felt I had the strongest pull to make a sexual connection.

It was Brad who actually scored first. He developed a relation-ship with this adorable, little, almost gingerbread-like girl from our class. She seemed so demure, with her brunette bob-cut always in place and her socks always colored and ruffled at the ankles (yes, I am talking about the late '80's here). And she seemed to be very quiet.

Then one day, we met up after school, and Brad seemed ready to explode. We walked to 6th Street to play basketball, and he was beaming from ear to ear. "What is your problem?" I asked. And the words all but rushed out of Brad's mouth, "I did it, I had sex with Susanne. And it was amazing!" I listened to this, frozen in shock. Silence fell upon us for a good 15 seconds before I bombarded him with questions. "What was it like? What did she do? What did you do? How did it feel? Where were you?" He was so pleased to be the first to answer these questions, and I was all too pleased to have someone to tell us about it. "I knew she was going to let me do it. We were upstairs in the TV room, laying on the couch watching TV," he said. I kept pressing in, my eyes feeling like they were about to bulge out of my head. "Then I took my hand and slipped it into her pants, and she didn't stop me!" he exclaimed with enthusiasm. The rest of the details had all of us standing with our jaws dropped.

As their relationship progressed, the stories got more detailed. Apparently, little Miss Susanne was a bit of a sex fiend. She was addicted.

A few weeks later, Brad pulled me aside, probably because I

validated his every move with my excitement to hear all the explicit movements, noises, and more of his first experience. He told me, "We snuck downstairs this weekend and put blankets behind the couch. Susanne screamed so loud this time, and I got super excited!" My mind was racing. I was wondering when my turn would come and how I could live out all of these fantasies I had created in my head. My body was throbbing inside, wanting to feel what I knew I had seen through the doors of my mother's bedroom and now experienced vicariously through the vivid images of Brad's escapades.

It wouldn't happen for me until I came home the next summer, fresh off the beaches of Florida. I had developed a blonde head of hair and a suntan that seemed worth its value in gold. As I came back into the reality of high school, I had no future aspirations, no goals, and no motivation until I met Liz.

Liz was a very pretty Portuguese girl, with long wavy hair that was normally styled high with hairspray. Our romance quickly developed into a very unhealthy relationship. I was aggressive with my desire to open the door for sex. I desperately wanted my own stories, my own feelings, and my own sexual experiences.

I was quickly consumed with sex and became overbearing and controlling. I was her first real boyfriend and remembered having to ask her father, Fred, if I could date his daughter. I stood there awkwardly at their front stoop, shifting my feet on the grit from the bricks beneath my sneakers. "Umm, hello, sir. I was wondering, um, if I could, um, date your, um, Liz?" I stammered. He just stood there staring down at me. My hair was gelled and spiked in bleached streaks from the sun. A smile crept over his face as he put out his hand.

Her parents knew that my parents were divorced, and they really took me in and made me part of their family. I was often at her home for dinners and was included in almost all of the family functions and trips. Despite their kindness, I would continuously push limits and abuse the trust and hospitality they so generously showed me.

Liz was my first live, sexual experience, and I was hers. Our first time trying was in her closet. She had made a bed with sheets on the floor. "Hmm, interesting," I had thought. I guess we were intimidated by the bed.

Nevertheless, it happened, and now something had been unleashed in me. I could not get enough. Yes, I know lots of teenaged boys are obsessed with sex, but I took it to a whole new level. I wanted sex from her all the time, everywhere, anywhere, almost every day after school in the alcove, behind the stairs, all over her house, sometimes just feet from her parents. It was absolutely crazy, and I was driving the ship. She went along with it, but I felt like I needed it.

It wasn't just sex, however. My need to control Liz infringed on her personal boundaries. The more time we spent together, the more and more I became unhinged. On several occasions, I snuck into her room and read her diary. I sat on her bed, reading her feelings, recounting how she was experiencing sex, and I felt gratified, yet completely out of control.

As the months flew by, I became more consumed with her than anything else around me. I was acting like a man, feeling like a boy, and caught in a delusion of grandeur. We continued having unprotected sex. My negligence and irresponsibility would never come to collect, thankfully. I just didn't understand or, more importantly, respect sex or how to treat women.

Her family became painfully aware of my controlling ways when they offered to host Liz's sweet sixteen birthday party, and I edited the invite list. I deprived this lovely and energetic girl a joyous celebration because of my own insecurities and immaturity. I have never forgotten that day. It represents an ugliness that I never wish to repeat.

SESSION 4: FORGE FORWARD

Unstructured and hopeless, I am totally on my way to flunking out of Bernardsville High School. The week before, my Dad and I drove past a homeless guy rummaging through a garbage can. Dad pointed at the guy and said to me, "Is this going to be you, Craig?"

I grimace. I have an aptitude for athletics, but my academics prevent me from participating consistently. No sense of duty, no sense of urgency. Why should I care, when life is full of disappointment?

Walking down the hall at school, I hear, "Craig, come with me now." Damn, what is it now, I think. Nothing good, I'm sure.

Coach LaSpada, the varsity soccer and wrestling coach strong-arms me into the athletic office to see Mr. Ferry. Mr. Ferry? The athletic director? But why does he want to see me?

No more time to think; I am in Mr. Ferry's office.

"Sit down," Coach LaSpada says, gesturing to a chair. I slump down in dread.

Mr. Ferry turns around in his office chair and looks at me. "Coach LaSpada has been telling me about you, Craig. Go on; I want to hear your story from you."

I start talking, barely making eye contact. "I love sports, but Coach

LaSpada won't let me participate because of my grades. I just can't bring them up. Nothing I do works."

I can tell from his expression that Mr. Ferry isn't having it. He doesn't mince words with me, nor is he open to my interpretation of my current academic and athletic situation. He stares intently at me and says, "Kid, do not say another word. I got a place for you."

Soon enough, I come to realize he is actually Lieutenant Colonel Donald Ferry of the United States Air Force. And I find out that the place he has in mind for me is Valley Forge Military Academy in Wayne, Pennsylvania.

Little do I know that by sending me to Valley Forge what Lieutenant Colonel Ferry is really doing is handing me a lifeline to a support system I have never had before. It will completely change my life.

Thirty Years Later

BATTLING WITH THE THOUGHT, "Am I really an alumni?" I return to Valley Forge. Though I am invited to present at Alumni Career Day, the first event for an entire weekend hosted by the school, I feel strange about it right from the start. The coordinator of the Alumni Weekend asks me to grab the IDs for all of the speakers. And of course, since I never graduated from Valley Forge, I don't have an ID. The guy who is pulling up pictures doesn't have mine, and he isn't going to because I don't have a senior picture. It is surreal. They run out of time, so I am saved from being discovered before I go to the first classroom presentation.

I am on the hook to do three presentations. In the first classroom, I fake it and pretend to be an alumni. It is really terrible. My thoughts are fractured, and I am extremely unclear. The students have no idea what I am talking about.

Walking away from the first classroom for a 40-minute break, I decide faking it is no longer going to work. At this point, right before *speaking to the second classroom, I decide to out myself as never having graduated.*

I walk in and start. My throat feels scratchy. "Good afternoon, cadets. Many of the alumni who are here today have lived lives of honor, great accomplishment, and service to others. I stand before you, representing none of these things in my life."

The cadets look surprised. I keep going.

"I never graduated. Take any message you want from this. Don't let fear run your life the way it did mine. I left early from this place, and I have regretted it every day of my life."

I realize as I present for the second and third classrooms that I have been living a lie. Once I admit it, I know I have just as important a role as the firefighter and the professor who come and speak. I tell my truth and just say, "Take what you want from this." I OWN IT. It has taken 30 years for me to out myself to myself.

Even though there is a catered meal for us in the banquet room, I go to the mess hall instead and eat by myself. I am no longer an alumni, and I cannot represent myself as one. I eat, sitting alone, watching the cadets enjoying their lunches together at the other tables lining the mess hall.

Even though this is the first event for the Alumni Homecoming Weekend, I head straight to the train and leave. I take my little brief-case, filled with crackers and a notebook, and walk across campus, following the weathered brick walkway. Exit stage right.

This was my last time entering campus pretending to be someone I wasn't. Saying it out loud, admitting, "I wasn't a great person; I didn't do great things in my life." Being the anti-hero means I am authentically being me, and finally owning my real experience at Valley Forge Military Academy, rather than the one I so much wanted to be true for both myself and my dad. I think my father would be proud that I owned up to it and took responsibility EVEN after all this time!

AFTER MY RELATIONSHIP with Liz crashed and burned, I complained a lot to my dad about how uncomfortable I was interacting at school. I had pushed away my group of friends while Liz and I were hot and heavy, and it left an aching discomfort at school. I was a horrible student right from the beginning and lacked the typical social qualities of a thriving teenager. I am not sure how it started or exactly when it became evident to my parents or teachers. I just never seemed to have the discipline and sense of importance about anything school-related. Looking back, it is somewhat alarming, but at the time, I was not aware in any sense of the word. I lacked any sense of urgency.

I can't remember a time when I felt comfortable in school, and I needed all kinds of help from guidance counselors and school aides to stay on track. "Craig, we have the same conversation every week. Why are you so distracted in class? How can we help you?" the guidance counselor asked as I stared blankly at her face. Her lacy blouse was a distraction, as I could almost see down the middle of her cleavage as she leaned toward me in compassion. With her blonde hair swept up in a bun, she was desperately trying to disguise her youth in a sea of elderly, highly-tenured teaching staff. "We will need to see more from you in order to pass you this year." I scoffed, thinking nothing of that warning.

It was tenth grade, and I was left back, having to complete the entire year over. "Daddy, I can't do it again, I hate it here," I told him. "Don't worry, Craig, let's find you a change of scenery," he said, lacking any anger or judgement. He seemed genuinely happy to find an outlet for me. We moved to Bernardsville, New Jersey, about a mile from my childhood home in Bridgewater.

Once I met Lieutenant Colonel Ferry, he connected me to my new school, Valley Forge Military Academy in Wayne, Pennsylvania. I arrived on the campus in the summer for a 3-week program for new cadets. My dad hugged me. "Craig, this is your chance, do it!" he exclaimed with genuine excitement in his thick voice. I threw my grey duffel bag on the mattress in my new room. The wood frames were spaced no more than a foot from one another, with two beds in a tiny room for two cadets. "I'll be here next weekend," my dad said, and then turned and exited the room. I made the bed with the hard, thin sheet set that was set out for me. Taking the bed furthest from the door, I lay down, putting my arms behind my head, and stared at the ceiling. My roommate arrived about 10 minutes later. He was quiet and embarrassed as his mom gave him a giant hug before his burly dad ushered her out of the room. We didn't speak — not one word. We were summoned to the auditorium for intake.

After our first few days of hardcore athletic training, I felt at home. Working my body to its capacity was invigorating. I quickly became a member of Bravo company as the new school year began. I did very well at the school academically. Something about being within the military structure made sense to me. Without the distraction of girls, I was able to channel my energy in a positive direction for the next 2 years.

This 2-year period was the only time I remember feeling any peace with my mom, Bernie, and my dad. No one fought when we all went out to eat together. And for the only time in my life, they seemed proud of me. It was the opiate of hope that I clung to, wanting to finally become something.

And I started making good on my desire. During my second year, and at the height of my success, I was chosen along with another cadet to represent our academy at a scholastic leadership workshop at the Valley Forge Freedom Foundation. There were student representatives from schools all over the country.

In my third year, I was elected to participate in OCS (Officer Candidate School), with an appointment as Executive Officer 1st Lieutenant of Bravo Company. As required, we reported for the month-long training program in August. I was terrified with fear from the start as my father dropped me off and left beaming with pride. He was so happy that I had turned things around and was going to be a leader in the school.

The OCS summer training session was in full swing with several cadets assigned as part of a temporary cadre in military leadership roles each morning as part of our practical education. I was terrified each day that I would be called on, and one day it was just too much. All of my insecurities came back, and I panicked.

I quickly went to my room. I grabbed a bag and ran away. I walked and walked, stopping at a nearby gas station. When my father got the call that I was headed home, he was absolutely devastated. I broke his heart and, ultimately, his spirit. He would never be the same, and I really felt a part of him died that day. As he picked me up, his eyes stared intently at the road. He didn't speak a word to me the entire ride back from the school.

I gave up a great opportunity, and this single event would haunt me for the rest of my life. What I hadn't realized is where I would be going next. My father had fallen out of sorts in his life during these years away and was now living in a men's rooming house in New Jersey. So I had no home to return to. I left military school and had to move back in with my mother. This news was almost as unbearable as the guilt, shame, and failure I was feeling from my departure. I was forced to return to the house where so much trauma had occurred, and now, practically a grown man, I moved back in.

I returned to public school. Since I was lacking in sufficient credits from Valley Forge, I was now 2 years behind. To make it worse, I was now matriculating with my younger sister's class. It was embarrassing, and I was humiliated, but I brought it on myself. I had few friends, fewer interests, and absolutely zero direction. I didn't fit in with the students, and the school staff didn't want anything to do with me. They just wanted to get me out of the school before I brought any more attention to my strange scenario, a 21-year-old high school senior. They just left me alone. I never took an exam or received a report card. Instead, I just walked into the school office at the end of the year and was summarily handed a folder with my diploma and transcripts. I was given a white glove pass and 'graduated,' clearly without earning it. Back then, I was appreciative and relieved. Now, I realize they were doing me a great disservice and essentially just wanted to wash their hands of me. Unfortunately for me, other than clear fraud I witnessed, it helped me to concretize a belief that I could circumvent the system and ignore rules and standards. It was a pattern I would perfect and use for years.

It would be another decision that would have no solution, no way to repair, and no way to go back. My mom would wake up each morning, sit with her coffee and paper at the table, and nod begrudgingly at me as I entered the kitchen.

By this time, my mom and Bernie had divorced, and she was back in the saddle with random men and dalliances. I was at an age where I was no longer interested in her sexual affairs, and she had grown more docile after her time with Bernie. I wished at times that she would welcome me home and show some signs of warmth, compassion, sympathy, or understanding. But it would never come.

During one of her 'sessions', a man asked my mom about the lump in her breast. She hadn't noticed it. After going to a doctor, she was referred to a specialist and was quickly diagnosed with Stage 3 breast cancer. They began aggressive treatment, and she subsequently underwent a mastectomy while I was still living with her. The whole process was surreal.

After the surgery, she needed care. "Craig, I need you to help me," she stated dryly. "Okay, Mommy," I replied. I helped her with her daily health needs and redressed her bandages throughout the day, as she didn't have the energy or agility to maneuver for a while. My heart truly felt for her. Her frail body and narrowing face were not filled with the same fire or fierceness of her past self. One positive was that she took a break from her selfish mother act, and let up somewhat on me. No hounding about the dishes or complaining. No feelings of uselessness or guilt for being under the same roof.

This time didn't last long. The year was quickly fleeing, and I had been so focused on my mom and getting through each day, that I had sidestepped post-high school planning. I realized that there wasn't much for me in terms of a future, wealth, success, or happiness. As the last year dwindled away, it would take one chance happening at the end of high school for those odds to swing my way finally.

SESSION 5: UN-MERRY MOUNT

Now with Valley Forge in the rearview mirror, I have to collect some needed credits. However, I am sick and tired of feeling embarrassed all the time and doomed to be in the same grade with my sister and kids my sister's age; I am broken. I can see it in their faces. They don't care if I pass, fail, or drop out. It isn't hatred. It is worse than that. What I see in their eyes is complete indifference.

Replaying in my head over and over are the words from the high school principal. He was talking with a teacher about me and my not-so-hot reputation. The principal spoke up. "Don't worry about Craig lying to you," he said to the teacher. "The only person Craig lies to is himself." I believed what they were saying, too.

As a mental get-away, I walk once again to Mr. Mark's office, my guidance counselor. Sitting in his khakis and sporting his typical comb-over, he is a total 'carbon-based douche', but at least offers a respite from my misery at school. Whenever I go to his office, he is the Ed McMahon to my Johnny Carson. Talking with him is where I discover my propensity for comedy and off-the-cuff wit. It's never really been about getting me on the right track. His office is just the only outlet I have. No matter what, he has to listen to me.

Sitting on Mr. Mark's beat-up sofa, I grab and flip through college brochures. Looking at the manicured college lawns and smiling students, I fantasize about something I can't have...going somewhere. Being someone. Doing something with my life.

Suddenly Mr. Mark's door is pushed open. A guy is looking at me like fresh meat. He is from Marymount University. When he says to Mr. Mark that he is hosting a college recruitment session, I get up and walk briskly out of the office. Not for me, I think to myself.

An hour later, I am shocked to hear my name over the intercom. "Craig Maltese, please report to the auditorium." Apparently, no one else had signed up to attend the college presentation, and since I am the warmest body they have, I was drafted. Later at a mixer, the Marymount soccer coach, Coach Moser, rushes up to meet me. Coach Moser champions my admission into the school with the caveat that I will be joining the team.

As I took my first steps across the Marymount University campus in Arlington, Virginia, I remember wondering, how did I actually pull off getting into college? With so many hiccups in high school, it never crossed my mind that I would be accepted to any other school in my future. The thought of being on a campus that enrolled 80% of female students was more than overwhelming. The only friend that I had ever developed by that time remained in our home town in New Jersey and would follow his father's footsteps into the family dentistry practice. We never kept in touch as I moved away. Although I've often thought about what I valued as success back then, I wondered: Would my friend consider his stepping into a family business fulfilling, or was he just walking the path that was in front of him? The confusion surrounding being accepted was indeed that - was it a miracle, or a curse?

I didn't know how to speak with people and shied away from all social interactions, including those at the cafeteria. Why was it every day I walked through there, I could feel people staring, girls giggling and pointing, and my face burning with the discomfort of not knowing a single person? My first roommate didn't last long, either. I'm not sure if it was him or me. "Hey man," he said to me on the first day, as I entered the dorm room. I nodded, and barely let out a grunt. That was the last piece of communication we had over the next few days. But one day, I got called into the office and told I was being reassigned to a different dorm.

By this time, I was regularly frequenting the grocery store, eliminating the need to visit the cafeteria or any other communal area on campus. I also found the campus weight room. It was about the size of a walk-in closet and smelled like a mix of body odor and mold. I would soon look for an alternative away from campus.

After being reassigned to a new building, I ventured to my new dorm room. It was incredibly solitary. Looking back, I realize it enabled my awkwardness and enhanced my isolation from others. It was an old building, and I could hear all the cars whizzing by outside, but there weren't a lot of other people on my floor. There was no sign of females within blocks of this building. We even had a special key that opened the elevator and took us directly to our floor. In retrospect, that would have been a great seller to the ladies for discretion.

The resident dorm assistant, Bill, took me under his wing and encouraged me to assimilate. "Craig, hey man, how is it going?" he asked as I came off the elevator. "Good," I said, trying to rush into my room. "What's the deal, Craig?" Bill asked, genuinely concerned. "I'm just not into being social," I said without regret. "I get it, man, I get it," he replied. "I just know it can be lonely in college. I want to make sure you know if you need anything, you can ask. I'm right down the hall," he said as he pointed to a door with an 'RA' plastered on the front of it. He meant it, too.

Through his encouragement, I found a local YMCA with a weight room. It became my escape, my refuge, and my strength when I didn't seem to have it in any other areas of my life.

Soccer was quickly becoming a distant existence. The team was filled with highly competitive players, and my years of ineligibility from high school left me far behind my teammates' skill level. With my impact becoming more irrelevant on the team, and my physical aptitude suffering from lack of practice, I dedicated my energy and time into exercising on my own. The YMCA quickly became a place of comfort, and the gym, albeit tiny, sufficed for my first year.

Finances were now tight. My dad had lost yet another job and was again living in a rooming home for men. In fact, it was the very same place he lived upon separating from my mother. He and my brother had lost their house due to poor financial decisions. My brother would never truly let go of this and blamed me for my dad's rash financial decisions, for which I am sure he lost his investment too.

I moved off campus for a sabbatical, or as they say now, 'gap year'. And I reunited with my Dad, moving into a room next to his in the rooming house. This was a very humbling time for me, but my father had accepted it. His life had been spent not knowing how to maintain success, and I looked externally, desperately, for a role model to come forth. We lived like this for a short period before I realized this was not the life I was going to sign up for. It had all been without thought and intention for the future, until this point, and I felt compelled to change it. This was not one of those holy moments, where the light bulb of epiphany emerges from the dark, but rather the cravings of a young man, wanting more from relationships. It would be years before I saw anything from that yearning.

New Year's Eve rolled around, and I sat while people watching. Young men and women were scurrying about, sporting tuxes and ladies in the salons getting their updos. I looked in the mirror. "What is your problem?" I asked myself. "Loser," the person in the mirror answered.

Never can I remember feeling so alone, isolated, or unwanted. These people had friends, and more importantly, purpose. I just wanted the opportunity to live life from inside the glass, not watching from outside. I began to lose motivation but confided in my Dad about my love of exercising in the gym and how it gave me a sense of purpose and peace.

However unexpected and out of character it was, my father stepped up to the plate. He built up enough gumption to walk into a local gym. Enter stage right, my first experience into 'real fitness'. He bought a membership for me and arranged to get me to the gym every day. I got into bodybuilding from that first day. As one of the smaller lifters at the facility, I knew if I were going to be comfortable, I would need to watch and learn. And I did just that.

I quickly wanted more out of my fitness time. My dad, the new and improved man with resourcefulness, approached the owner and said, "My son is lost and wants to do something in fitness." The owner, Ron, agreed to train me. I still think it was the despair in my father's voice that created such compulsion in Ron to work with me. And for that, I will always be grateful.

The guys at the gym were ruthless. I was made fun of for my outfits, lack of large muscles, and technique. After hours and hours spent working, sweating, and not giving up, I earned the respect of the other bodybuilders. And it was my first time feeling a sense of camaraderie. Second only to my desire to be wanted by a woman, I had an intense craving to be accepted that haunted me throughout my life.

Once I started exercising regularly and feeling more confident, I took out a loan to return to school. I knew at this point no college gym or local Y would do. I found a Gold's Gym near the campus, just like I had seen in all the bodybuilding magazines I read as a teenager. It was a large, open space with machines and iron everywhere. I would eventually call this place my home.

As another college holiday came, I remember not knowing where my Dad or Mom were. No one reached out. I had lost contact with my sister during college, and my older brothers had their own lives. Unmotivated to be surrounded by family and plagued by not being able to keep up with the loan requirements, I knew my options were minimal. With the dorms closing, I had to figure out someplace to stay, and fast. The college collections officer, Rob, knew me very well by now, and had given another one of his regular calls. When he found out I wasn't able to go anywhere for the holiday, I spent Thanksgiving with him and his family.

It was a strange time for me. My resentment in not having anyone to count on was growing, but I directed it at the one thing I knew was constant, the gym. I had begun working at Gold's Gym, doing odds and ends around the facility to pay for a membership; stocking shelves, cleaning, racking weights, taking messages. As I continued to show progress in learning and speaking up, the boss, Bruce, gave me a better paying position. He asked what my deal was and upon finding out I was struggling and not happy with life on campus, he offered to give me steady part-time shifts in the gym. The excitement of being a part of the staff was incredible. I felt high on life and knew that I could see myself here for a while.

While I was getting my feet wet, my dad was getting another blow to the bank from his former wife, my mother. She was selling the house, and by default of the law, he was entitled to half of the proceeds. She convinced him to sign over his half to her. She knew his weakness was his kids. She manipulated that angle with a verbal agreement that she would use his half to give over to my sister and me to help us through college. My dad still loved my mom. He never truly understood the depth of her selfishness. He obliged and signed the agreement. After the closing, she collected every last dime herself and moved to Florida.

She began to spend the money immediately. It was non-stop. She bought cars and fixed her teeth. She even purchased the kind of fancy, uncomfortable furniture that no one could sit on or touch, and a house to put it all in. Before long, she had created a material world that only she could enjoy. She quickly spent all of it.

It was shortly after this that her health took a final hit, as her cancer returned and metastasized. As a late twenty-something, I quickly became very responsible and shed my resentment in order to support her. She was my mom, and I wanted to help.

I bought a bus ticket and headed down to Florida to be with her. The cancer had spread; it was extremely aggressive and would take her life very quickly. Upon my arrival, her lack of enthusiasm for my presence was evident. I didn't have much to offer other than company, and the ability to be of physical assistance with helping her in and out of bed, refreshing her water, and getting anything she needed that wasn't within reach. As a few days passed, sitting in the hospital with her, I wished we had a better connection, to be able to talk with one another. I had compassion, but it was rare that I had an opportunity to exercise it. My mother did not make this any easier.

The time came when I had to head back to Virginia while she was still hospitalized, but our parting conversation imprinted in my mind. She told me that she didn't want to hear from me unless I had good news. To be more exact, she said, "I don't want contact unless you have something good to say." She didn't want to be a part of my misery, my discomfort in life, or be privy to any of my tribulations. She made it clear that she only wanted the bouquets, which were hard to come by at that time for me. I sat on the bus, confused at how my visit had ended this way. The seed for discontent was planted. Relationships were skewed, and love was not a strong word that would enter my brain during the next decade.

The last time I would see her, she would be lying in a hospice facility, almost lifeless, unable to communicate with my siblings or me. This once vibrant woman, full of vigor, lay dying, bloated, and hallucinational as we all said our last goodbyes.

SESSION 6: A GOLD'EN TIME

I avoid eating in the cafeteria at Marymount. No confidence, no social skills, no friends on campus means the only time I feel any self- assurance is at the gym. It is my only solace. And John, a trainer at the gym, a very smart, charismatic, and highly educated man, is my only friend. I move in with him as his roommate. While he seems nice on the surface, I notice some strange behaviors.

John's primary personal training client is Mary, a kind, overweight, middle-aged woman. I notice that they spent a lot of time together, both at and away from the gym. Today, Mary and John are arguing. John yells upstairs for me to come down. When I come downstairs, she pouts, points her finger at John, and says, "Go ahead."

John, looking determined, turns to me, looks me in the eye, and says, "Sheffy, I am having sex with Mary for money."

Then he turns back to face Mary. "See, Mary, I told him. Don't ever threaten me."

I know right away how John wants me to respond, so I do. I just casually walk upstairs like, "Whatever dude." I glance back briefly to see she is staring at him in horror.

John, Mary, and I have no idea how all of this will eventually unfold and self-destruct. How could we not have seen it?

AFTER RETURNING BACK TO SCHOOL, I began to dive into the gym every waking hour I could. In my mind, I needed something good to happen, some escape from my imposed reality. Whether it was working, cleaning, lifting, or watching others' technique and form, I was obsessed. Roughly 6 months passed, and I was promoted to fitness counselor. My job was to orient new members through a 12-piece exercise circuit. I would fill out a program card for them, noting their seat and weight settings to allow for trackable results. I really enjoyed it, and for the next several months, I would work 4 to 5 days a week doing both front desk and new member orientation sessions.

"Follow me through here, watch your step," I said to a lively couple. "To your right is where you'll find our free weights, and over here, you will find our circuit training section," I said with authority. "In the back corner is our boxing equipment with a heavy bag and speed bag," I continued as I pointed to the far corner of the gym.

I was comfortable speaking with these members, working with them through this concise program, with all the scripts on-call throughout our interactions. To me, this made sense; this was a positive interaction for me and good practice. The older trainers and seasoned staff took every opportunity to poke fun at my enthusiasm for doing the most mundane tasks. It hurt me tremendously because I desperately sought their approval and respect. The gym and this job were really all I had going for me, so I pushed through it. School was no longer of interest, and I continued to become more detached. Over time, however, the gym staff would eventually let up and allow me some peace of mind.

The ownership team was a no-nonsense group of four guys not much older than me, but who were far more mature. They were a true fitness dream team led by the one and only Captain (as he was known by staff and members alike). He indeed was a captain, a born leader, and a powerful role model. He was loud, obnoxious, and pushy, but also funny and incredibly motivated to make it in the fitness business. I liken him to a charismatic bully, with a distinct hopping walk that matched his high energy. When he entered the gym, no matter where you were within the thousands of square feet of the facility, you would know he had arrived!

I naturally gravitated to this bravado. His ability to dominate the room empowered me. I would practice this in my head when I went home at night, having imaginary conversations with staff, and watching their faces react to my grandiose demeanor.

His brother, Jack, the polar opposite of the Captain, was very unassuming, calm, and easygoing. They were two of the four partners who helped balance one another well. I didn't fully realize that until later into my own management years. The other partners found their way into fitness through roles in commercial real estate and finance, but they also brought a solid knowledge of business operations and technology. Jeff was a hybrid of chief information officer and chief financial officer. He was all business, focused, very smart, very charming, but also very cold at times, a serious numbers guy. The last piece of the puzzle was Bruce. He had a background like the Captain, in commercial real estate. He was charismatic and a smooth talker.

The team continued to open facilities throughout Northern Virginia, Southern Maryland, and Washington, D.C. Within a few years, they had become by all accounts and financial metrics the largest and most successful fitness franchise group in the area, and I was a part of it, right there in the thick of it!

I remember my father coming back into my life during this time and being impressed with Bruce. He would comment to me on how well Bruce carried himself, his manners, ambition, professionalism, success, and determination. Bruce was only a few years older, but he was leagues above where I was on the map of maturity, poise, and self-confidence. My father wanted so much for me to take Bruce's lead, adopt this new mentor, and skyrocket to unknown successes. He would often ask me, "Are you going to be somebody one day, Craig?"

Within a year of working there, I was called into the office by the Captain. I entered the office, his long skinny legs covered by black Perfetto brand sweatpants atop his desk, fanny pack around his waist, leaning back in his chair. He expressed his appreciation for my work over the last several months and told me that they were opening two new gyms. One was going in a former supermarket, a huge 2-floor location, and the other was moving into a smaller location in a bustling commuter hub, about one mile from each other. I was offered a role on the big team!

I was summarily assigned to the smaller location, where I worked in concert with Bruce in the pre-sale office. I was a part of every aspect of the Rosslyn location's development. I was included in every stage of the year-long process, from construction, membership sales, equipment layout, and design of the steam room, flooring, lockers, and more. I spent almost every day with Bruce, modeling his sales techniques, his mannerisms, the way he sat, the way he smiled, everything. I really looked up to him, and at that time, he represented everything I wanted to be. He was handsome, intelligent, successful, smart, charming, tough, shrewd, and generous. Make no mistake, however; he meant business.

He taught me how to sell, he coalesced my growth, and in many ways put me together as a person. We continued to work side by side in a very close space throughout the several months it took to open the gym. Once the gym opened, Bruce assumed his role as general manager and managing partner, and I became a full-time team member. My primary job was to sell memberships and oversee the maintenance of the facility. The goal was always to close at least two deals (memberships) a day. I was good at my job, but at times my growing compulsion to exercise pulled me away from my membership sales responsibilities. In Bruce's eyes, being on the gym floor hindered my ability to sell new memberships. In fact, I can remember several times when Bruce would pull me off the gym floor during my workout after my shift because I didn't hit two deals for the day. It was not a right to exercise there, it was a privilege, and you had to earn it, EVERY DAY!

I had my ups and downs with Bruce, periods when I was

engaged and selling a lot of memberships, and times when I wasn't. Mostly, it was countless hours of self-indulgent exercising, my extracurricular entrepreneurial ambitions, and my ongoing prurient shenanigans that would ultimately be my undoing. And it would be a long time until that very cycle would break.

During this time, there was only one certified trainer in our Rosslyn location, and his name was John. He had a solid following and was an excellent trainer with incredible charisma. He was a big personality and a big man. He was about 6'2, 250 lbs, African-American, and looked like a defensive lineman in the NFL.

John lived in a large townhouse directly behind the gym and had a room he was looking to rent. I jumped on the opportunity and moved into the top floor with an ensuite bathroom. John and I spent a great deal of time both at home and at work together over the next year and a half.

Oddly enough, we never really invested emotionally in each other. We had a lot in common, including our shared fitness experience and both being from New Jersey. But we never really connected on a deeper level. We were just two guys on the same path. He really was a great guy, very kind, very generous, very smart, but he was no pushover. John did not like confrontation, and at the time, I didn't either, so we did not argue at all. John had always said about me, "He lets me be me."

Gold's Gym is where I received my nickname, Sheffy. Seven of us at the gym were named Greg or Craig, so it became confusing. John mentioned that he thought I looked like the actor Craig Sheffer and started calling me Sheffy. Since we would get paged over the intercom to meet with clients at the gym, calling out for 'Sheffy' eliminated confusion.

When I wasn't hanging around with John, I spent time with Travis. He was the first person I ever signed up for a gym membership in the Rosslyn pre-sale office. Travis was in law school at the time in D.C., and while he was very smart, he was also very rough around the edges, a loner like me. I could relate to him in that way. We became full-time training partners. He was not well-liked by

John or Bruce, but we got along. One night I met him at his tiny, very messy studio apartment to grab dinner. I walked in and immediately noticed a large handgun on a table in the center of his apartment. He saw me react and asked if I would like to hold it. I did. I remember how heavy it felt. It was the first and last time I would ever hold a gun. Travis was a force to be reckoned with, and he had no fear. I knew I would find myself in a bad situation if we continued hanging out. I focused most of my time with him working out and playing video games. I began to limit my time with Travis shortly after the incident with the gun and showed more interest in spending time with John.

One of John's favorite shows was the soap opera, "General Hospital". I kind of got into it too, though I rarely admitted it. Nevertheless, this one weekday afternoon, I was home watching it, and John rang me. In the days of landline phones, you had to be home to receive calls. It was one conversation I will never forget. "Sheffy, get your ass down here, man. I'm at Camelot's. I've got a table filled with strippers waiting for us," he said as he clicked his mouth in a gesture of confidence. I don't remember hanging up the phone. I was off the couch and out the door as quick as my legs could carry me.

I ran across the Key Bridge to Georgetown and caught a taxi to Camelot's in the heart of Washington D.C. True to his word, John was there at 3:30 pm on a weekday afternoon sitting at a corner table in a darkened room surrounded by a bevy of strippers. I didn't know it then, but strippers and sex would become an ongoing theme in my life. For now, though, it was the most exciting feeling I can remember. I no longer felt regret for not connecting with any of the girls at my college campus. I mean, really, I thought, how could they compare to the hottest girls you have ever seen? Besides, the girls on campus, though very nice, were mostly Northeastern prep-school girls with Band-Aids on their knees from years of playing the cello.

I was thrilled with my new group. We ate lunch that day in the strip club, steak and yellow rice. I won't ever forget that meal. We left and promised the girls we would be back, and we held tightly to those words.

John continued doing very well with personal training, and he was still a one-man show. In the spring of that year, an overweight woman in her mid-40's walked in and bought a membership that would shape the course of all three of our lives. Mary, a divorced mother of two, lived at home with her kids, elderly mother, and mentally challenged sister. She had a solid corporate job, drove a bright blue Camaro, and was clearly motivated to improve herself by joining a gym. Since John was the only trainer, he conducted her fitness orientation with the goal of obtaining her as a client. He had no idea what this seemingly unassuming middle-aged mother would be bringing to the table.

Shortly after their initial fitness orientation, Mary purchased a modest package of training sessions. They began a fitness program consisting of three sessions per week. After a few months and a few more training packages, I noticed that John wasn't returning home until much later in the evenings. One day I asked him about it, and he said that Mary had been taking him out to eat almost every day after they finished their sessions. The very next day, he invited me out with them. We went to a local Bennigan's, and we chowed down. At that time, I was a voracious eater and ordered steak, baked potatoes, rice, and dessert. I ate it all, as did John. He was naturally a big guy, and we both realized how fortunate we were. We made the most of Mary's generosity. Well, took advantage of it would be a more accurate description.

Throughout the entire summer, John and I were splitting time between the gym, strip club visits, and spending time with Mary. It got to the point where Mary was paying money directly to John instead of the gym. And they weren't exercising nearly as much inside the gym. What developed was a very co-dependent, dysfunctional, unprofessional, and dangerous relationship. A relationship that was supposed to be about Mary losing weight, increasing her self-esteem, and improving her overall quality of life, turned into a relationship that was none of those things.

John was loving the freedom and power he got from this extra money, and this power dynamic. He was literally billing Mary for hours spent with him doing whatever he wanted to do: watching TV, shopping, playing video games, eating, etc. This was the time when John told me he was having sex with Mary as part of that arrangement. Of course, I didn't get it then, but in retrospect why else would she agree to that lopsided deal? This continued for several months. By this time, in addition to their ongoing sex for money and time arrangement, she leased a car for John, a new red Mazda sports car. Up until that point, she had been letting us drive her second car, an ugly, beat-up sky blue minivan. It wasn't pretty, but it got us around. This is when we both fell further into the stripper scene. For me, however, it would be a much deeper downfall.

With hot new wheels and financing from Mary, we were on our way. By this time, too, I had moved more into personal training and almost entirely away from membership sales, and from Bruce's supervision. I had acquired a big client as well. He was a referral from John, which he would hold over my head from that moment on. Teddy, my client, was a college student at nearby American University in D.C. from a wealthy family. Teddy was hellbent on being a bodybuilder, his lack of sufficient genetics notwithstanding. Despite his lack of natural ability, I took him on as a client, and we trained several times a week. He was my first personal training client and the only one I had for the next year. He paid cash and was willing to do whatever it took to get big.

"Craig, so, umm, yeah man, what do you think about, uhh, ya know, gettin' some umm, steroids?" he sputtered. "You want me to get steroids for you!?" I tried to clarify without sounding accusatory. I knew where to get them, but up until that point hadn't had much experience other than my own occasional cycles of taking the milder steroids. I certainly hadn't sold any up to that point. But I just couldn't pass up the money and knew if I didn't come through on this, I would lose Teddy to another trainer who would.

It was a done deal. "Sure. I got you," I came back to him. I supplied Teddy with the best drugs I could find and reaped the reward. I acquired the drugs through a fellow trainer at our other gym up the street. There were many days I would inject him in his chauffeured car before or after our training session. I did whatever it took to maintain my lifestyle and provide Teddy with what he wanted.

On one particular night, John and I went to a strip club on Wisconsin Avenue called Good Guys, as we did on most nights. It was early evening, maybe 5 or 6 pm. We had gotten into the habit of eating our meals at strip clubs. We walked in, grabbed a table, and ordered dinner. I happened to have a newspaper on me, so John and I split up the paper and began reading it. The strippers were stunned! They were thinking, 'Who are these guys coming into a strip club ordering food and reading a newspaper while we are dancing nude?' Did I mention that these clubs were fully nude? The strippers were not used to this kind of behavior, so we stood out.

We spent the next couple of hours eating dinner, reading the paper. What we did not do, the entire time we were there, was look up at the stage. The girls were all over us and not in that fake 'WE WANT YOUR MONEY' way. It was more like, 'We want to take the other guys' money, and hang out with you two.' With their reaction, John and I thought we were on to something.

The next night we went back to Camelot's. Following our newfound standard operating procedure, we entered, ordered food, and read the newspaper. After 15 minutes or so, we had three girls at our table, one of whom was a cute little blonde girl (and by girl, I do mean 18 or older). We talked briefly at our table before her turn came to dance. From the moment she left the table, until the moment she returned two songs later, I never even looked up. She rolled right up to me when she returned to our table and said in somewhat of an annoyed tone, "You didn't even watch me dance." I said, "Well, I'm sorry, but I am sure you were great up there." That was it; I had her. In her world, nobody looked away. I did the exact opposite of what she expected and what everyone else was doing. I knew right then we were going to have a blast.

I thought at the time that John and I had completely changed the power dynamic with the strippers. Looking back now, I realize those girls leveraged the stupidity in our ruse with the newspaper. John and I didn't have any special gifts. The girls just loved needing to get our attention as it offered some much-needed variety from the typical customer experience to which they had become so accustomed.

It was still summer, and I was flush with money and free time. I picked up the cute blonde stripper the next Friday night after her shift at Camelot's. It was nearly 3 am and she was hungry, so we went to an all-night diner near my place. I don't even remember ordering my meal. I wasn't thinking about food. My mind was very preoccupied; I was already storyboarding the next few hours of sex I hoped to have.

Soon enough, there we were at my place. We had just eaten, and there wasn't much reason to leave the room for the foreseeable future. We ultimately wouldn't leave the room until about 16 hours later. When I eventually emerged, I had absolutely no idea what time or day it was. I remember coming into the living room where John and Mary were, getting some water and food, and going back to my room. My 'stripper friend' had a large stash of cocaine that kept her going. I had a mountain of failure with women that drove me; we each had our motivation. We remained in the room until late the next day. Then I took her to eat once more, and dropped her at her home.

When she had mentioned that she was scheduled for breast augmentation surgery the following week, I offered to help her with her doctor and hospital visit. Why wouldn't I? I was looking forward to being on the business end of her boob job. I felt it was the least I could do after the effort she showed me in the last few days. I did indeed help her through that process and was happy to do it. Unfortunately, I would not be able to get to know the very boobs I helped bring into the world. Our relationship was very volatile and was really only meant for a short time. I'm grateful it didn't last, as it just might've killed one or both of us.

Later, I would find myself on frequent, late-night cocaine runs when I was mingling with these strippers, as it was a go-to activity for them, one that opened the door for some 'horizontal refreshment' for me at any time of day. Now looking back I ask, why would I put myself in that kind of danger?

The stripper episode did not help me to learn to connect or communicate better with women in any way. If anything, it made me even more dysfunctional and detached. Stripper sex is by no means a good foundation for a healthy sexual or intimate relationship with a woman. This challenge added to the issues I already had from the flawed years of living with my mother, Bernie, and other preprogrammed shortfalls.

SESSION 7: DUCK, DUCK, GOOSE

When Goose picks me up at the gym, he has "Getting Jiggy Wit It" by Will Smith blasting in his car. Goose is a great dancer and starts moving to the bass. I really want to be like my friend. I start mimicking his moves a little, but as usual, I look and feel awkward. Goose has rhythm. I don't. I have no moves and definitely no finesse. Goose sees me, laughs, turns, and says, "Sheffy, you are a no-rhythm mofo." My heart sinks because I know he's right.

I want to change. I want to be like Goose. I watch Will Smith's video over and over, and I practice the same moves as the dancers. I sing along to the refrain..."Na na na na na na-na!" I'm not very agile, and my 5' 7", stocky stature is not supporting rapid body movements needed to follow the choreography. But I am determined.

When Goose and I get together again, "Getting Jiggy Wit It" comes on, and it is time. I move a little bit and show off my moves.

Goose is amazed. "Sheffy!!" he says, his voice peaking to show his approval.

From that point forward, that song is part of our bond. Goose and I now have a code word for when we decide to go rogue and head to the casino. Goose calls into the front desk at the gym, and leaves me a message: "Na na na na na na-na!" When I hear that message, I know it's game on.

On this day, Goose's call comes into the front desk. "Na na na na na na-na! 7 pm." On schedule at 7, he picks me up, and we head to the casino. But unlike most nights when Goose would play, and I would watch until sunrise, on this night Goose is really tired. He wants to leave while it is still dark and asks me to drive home. The thing is, I don't have a driver's license.

Undeterred at first, I drive us home from Bicycle Club Casino in Bellflower, California, to Newport Beach, which is about a 45-minute drive. I am so relieved when I realize we are nearly home. But then as soon as I have that thought, I see flashing blue lights in the rear-view mirror. I feel like my heart has stopped. And we are only about a block from my house!

As the cop walks to my side of the car, sweat breaks out on my forehead. What the hell am I thinking? The cop leans into my opened window.

"Good evening, gentlemen. Do you know why I pulled you over?" It turns out Goose's left tail light is broken. As I am panicking, Goose speaks up calmly.

"Hey Officer, I was just really tired. Okay, my buddy doesn't have a license. It was a one-time thing. It won't happen again."

Goose does it. The cop lets us go and warns Goose to get the light fixed. On the surface, I am relieved. But underneath, I know better.

Being with Goose means always being susceptible to trouble. Morally, I know he is putting me into bad positions. But with luck, and good timing, I still get off. How long can this last? My conscience keeps saying, "If you keep doing this, you're going to get into serious trouble." But I've become so dependent on the confidence I have around him that I push those feelings away. Deep down, I know this is a foreshadowing. Getting pulled over by the cop is going to be just the tip of the iceberg.

Eventually, I learn my gut has been telling me the truth. Just when you think you are safe with Goose, you aren't really safe at all.

MY LIFE HAD TAKEN a steep downward turn. John and Mary's relationship devolved in step with my career. Sex, money, and the initial flair of their relationship had peaked and quickly digressed as funds, attraction, and infatuation fell flat. This left Mary even more vulnerable than when she started. Not only did John take advantage of her emotionally, but ended the relationship with financial implications that wreaked havoc in her life.

I had stopped participating positively at work, took full advantage of the facility, and avoided authority and structure with the all-in intention to continue down this self-destructive path. What I had not realized was I had begun to value John's model more than that of my previous mentor, Bruce. I was training clients and not paying the requisite training fees to the club. Eventually, Bruce confronted me. His disappointment was palpable; he was hurt. I asked myself, "What does it mean to be somebody? Why can't I do anything right?" Haunted by my dad's desire for me to make something of myself, I remember the shame I felt and made a choice to run away.

I had very little going for me at this time. Having all but lost the once-solid relationship with Bruce, I lost both a mentor and all sense of direction. I was confused about who I was and who I wanted to be. Was I really interested in a legitimate fitness career or something else entirely? My sordid, shifty life, both inside and outside the gym, had cost me all the positive traction I had made, and I needed a fresh start. In addition, my primary client and major source of income had dried up, which it always eventually does. We were ultimately tired of one another. He stopped making progress as I knew he would, as his frame couldn't support the build he was looking to achieve. He left at the end of the semester, and I never saw or heard from him again. It was definitely time to move on. I didn't have the maturity to see things as they were and make positive headway.

In the spring, I left Virginia and moved to Southern California. I sold my furniture to John to pay my way, leaving him with over a thousand dollars in unpaid bills that came in after my departure. I moved in temporarily with my brother Dino, my sister and his girl-

friend (now wife), and my Dad. By this time, my father was diagnosed with terminal pancreatic cancer, and they were all helping
with his care.

I arrived in Orange County, California, wearing my Perfetto
brand 'body-builder' pants, a large T-shirt, and a branded gym
fanny pack. It's not a good look in any time period. I was still quite
'beefy' then and did not represent the Orange County, 'lean, mean'
fitness scene of that time.

Arriving jobless, I figured the easiest income generator would
be to obtain a personal training position with a local fitness chain. I
walked up to the front desk of a fitness club in trendy Huntington
Beach and asked for the fitness manager. A blonde, tan, thin,
athletic guy walked over from the fitness desk. He combed my
entire look and was noticeably agitated by my appearance. He
refused to interview me. I guess my buff bod was a bit too much for
the cool coastal clientele. Who knows. He recommended I go to
their Newport Beach location. There, my appearance was fortu-
nately not as offensive and I was hired on the spot.

While I had a seemingly short 2-year stint at this job, it was here
that I would meet Phil and Goose, both of whom would have a
significant impact on my life, in very different ways!

It was very early in the morning sometime during the first
month I was working at the Newport Beach gym on 19th St. This
particular morning, the front desk person was late, and a crowd
had gathered outside. Moments later, a figure appeared out of the
shadows. He was a bald-headed, African-American man on a bike.
I was surprised to see a middle-aged black man, on a bike, in
Newport Beach, which is a wealthy and predominantly white area
of California. I wasn't the only one shocked, as most of the faces of
the disgruntled bystanders in front of the club had comical looks of
confusion.

He quickly opened the doors and haphazardly checked-in the
irritated members without much emotional interchange. His name
was Kevin but called himself "Goose", a moniker his karate teacher
gave him years ago because he said he moved like a goose. I had a

hard time picturing it, too, so I guess his teacher must have seen some highly talented geese where they lived.

Kevin was a 10th-degree black belt in karate. He was charismatic, charming, and supremely talented. He was living with his longtime girlfriend, Brenda, in her apartment about a mile from the gym. He had spent close to 20 years in the Marines and was not short on confidence. He felt and truly believed he could do anything he wanted and did until he didn't any longer. But we will get there a bit later.

Once I had the finances to make a move, I did. I was able to afford a small apartment that I knew would offer me some privacy and a different landscape. There was a lot of friction during this time between my Dad and me, and he had noticeably given up on me. He told me that "all of the immigrants out here are more successful than you." My brother's steadiness and consistency were shining more brightly in my father's opinion, and I wasn't showing any visible upward trajectory. It had left them both frustrated with me. My sister was getting divorced from her first husband, and my brother Dino funded her until she got her finances and career back on track.

I quickly shifted my attention from matters of family back to my fitness life once again. Goose had started in membership sales but soon moved to personal training. He was very successful at training and very quickly began to enjoy the fruits of his labor. Unfortunately for him, having a successful business didn't help him the way it does for most people. He was a degenerate gambler, and his game was PAN 9, an Asian card game very similar to baccarat. We spent many full, late nights, gambling together at the Bicycle Club Casino, among others, just north of Orange County. He took gaming very seriously, and I just enjoyed his company, observing him and feeding off the excitement of the environment. For him, it was addictive; he just could not stop.

As his personal training career had opened up more avenues, he began meeting and subsequently dating more women. Four women, to be exact, three of whom he impregnated over an 18 month time period, including his long-time girlfriend Brenda, a school teacher from South Africa, and an Asian woman who owned a local restaurant. His penis was indeed an equal opportunity provider. With so many new variables in play, he left the gym and resumed his karate teaching career in a dojo, 100 percent funded by the parents of his students. As Kevin said to me many times, "All I have to do is teach these kids karate, and that's it. I love it." For Kevin, however, it still wasn't enough. It was never enough! He continued to gamble and in doing so, jeopardized all of his relationships, his position in the dojo, as well as his personal and professional finances. He allowed the karate dojo to devolve and eventually it closed due to his derelict supervision. He would later tell me that the reason he started gambling was to compete with the parents of the kids from the dojo. He had felt completely insecure and could not control his feelings of inadequacy, constantly comparing himself to their financial status.

Sometime, VERY soon after, I received a call from Brenda telling me Kevin had been arrested for breaking and entering and robbery. He was detained in the Orange County Jail in Santa Ana, and she said he urgently wanted to speak with me.

The next day I went to Brenda's apartment and awaited Kevin's collect call. He told me that this was all a big mistake, and he asked me to testify that I was with him the night he was arrested to back up his story. I wanted to help him. Although I was so impressionable and still a deep admirer of him, I knew I had been misguided. Knowing there was no way I could do that, I turned down his plea with great sadness and a heavy heart, and said that I couldn't offer him assistance. Again, I heard the disappointment in his voice.

Soon after, I resented him for trying to put me in that position, and the potential risks he was opening me up to, like perjury! His case went to trial; he was convicted and received 25 years to life. His long sentence length was ruled on account of the three-strike rule in the state of California. He has been incarcerated since 1998. He is indeed supremely talented and could really have done anything he wanted to. He had the guts, the charm, and the drive.

Kevin's disease wasn't really gambling; it was an infectious ego. A narcissistic way of life allowed him to believe that he could do whatever he wanted, whenever, wherever, to whomever, and somehow, some way, always get away with it. He believed he could keep living that way because he had gotten away with that behavior for so long. That was his downfall, believing his disproportionate reality! I think about how I idolized him, and how I just sat and absorbed all that he did. I am thankful that on the many nights I was out with him, driving in his car, stopping at this house and that house, I didn't become an accessory because I could have easily wound up like him. Looking back now, I realize that every single time I was with him, I was ALWAYS in the wrong place at the wrong time! I believed him and trusted him, and that was a mistake. Luckily, I escaped without any real damage, other than great sadness and bearing witness to a genuine waste of talent.

Back at the Maltese family estate, also known as my brother's house, my sister had saved up money to move herself and my father out to a tiny cottage on nearby Balboa Island. My father was declining fast. His days had always been numbered, but he continued on long after the doctor's prognosis. By this time, I was regularly visiting him. I remember the day the visiting hospice nurse said he wouldn't make it another day. I wanted to stay, but my brother told me to go home as he had continued to defy the doctors' death forecasts. When I called the next morning, a nurse answered, I asked where my dad was, and she answered, "They took him." I replied, "What do you mean they took him?" She then realized who I was and told me that he had passed. I sat stunned on the phone, unable to hang up the receiver. It just couldn't be true that he had passed away and I wasn't there. I kept replaying his voice, "Craig, you need to become somebody." I wanted to yell to him, "Dad, I will, one day, I will." But that was the farthest thing from the truth, as I had no idea what my future was going to bring. I wished that fact was different, that I had been able to tell him that with confidence I was somebody, before he died.

After about an hour of reeling over the news, I returned to the cottage. I remember seeing his watch and wallet on the table next to his bed. I completely broke down, sobbing, tears falling over my face, and my body shaking with total despair. I felt the fear, the emotion, the sadness that I never amounted to what he had wanted me to become, and all of these feelings poured out of me. I was devastated and overcome by the reality that I'd never see him again. Not being a traditionally emotional person, this reaction was foreign to me. I realized I'd never been able to be more than what I was at the moment to him, and that he died feeling like I was a loser. The night before, he had leaned forward toward me before I left the apartment and said, "Don't be afraid, it's OK; there is nothing to be afraid of." I don't know what he meant by that, but that moment still resonates vividly in my head. I never got to know him while I was an adult, after I stepped out of the childish excuses of my past. It's something I have struggled to come to terms with over the years, and still do! The loss of Goose and my father in a span of 6 months was devastating, and at that time I was even more lost and disillusioned.

We called my grandmother, who flew in with my aunt, who was my father's younger sister. My brother Dino, sister, aunt, and grandma boarded a boat and took a trip off the shore. We collectively threw my father's ashes off the side and out to sea. I remember hearing her say, "One should never have to see your child's life end before yours." Her withered face brought so much emotion back to the forefront. My father's death really crushed her. As I got to spend a few days with my grandmother, I remembered some of the best times in my childhood. We had the opportunity to reminisce about my summer visits at her condo, my mischief, and my attitude. Enjoying the stories of the past helped us connect back to happier times.

SESSION 8: PHIL-THY

The night begins with Phil trying to lift my spirits. He knows I'm down on myself for consistently striking out with women. I feel insecurity creeping through my mind. It isn't that I'm off my game. It's that I have no game. He genuinely likes being around me and often comments on how 'funny' I am. I am his comic relief. Phil hatches a plan to build my confidence.

"Sheffy, I'm gonna go see Coco tonight. She'll be down for something, you up for this?"

What do I have to lose? "Sure," I say.

As soon as Phil and I get to Coco's apartment building, we head straight to the pool. There is a hot tub there, already bubbling. I turn around, and there's Coco. She's a petite Asian, twenty-something-year-old girl, and I can hardly stop staring at her tiny bikini top. I keep looking away, feeling incredibly awkward. Unfazed, Phil begins taking everything off down to his boxer briefs. I look at him, and he looks back like he is saying, "Sheffy, get with the program."

I strip down to my boxer briefs too, and then all three of us get in the hot tub together. Although it is built for a number of people, on this night, the hot tub feels way too small. I cannot stop staring at Coco's breasts, and I am acutely aware of how awkward I am feeling. Her tiny red and blue polka-dotted bikini barely covers each nipple. It is in severe danger of jumping out and giving us a show, right here in the hot tub.

Then I see Phil reaching his hand down under the water. Wow, this hot tub is way too small, I think. Coco is just eating up the attention, giggling, and shifting closer to Phil. "I seriously do not belong here," I keep thinking. I start sweating and feel anxious as Phil starts kissing Coco's neck and removes the at-risk bikini top. The small inch of fabric that has been covering her chest is now gone.

Phil looks up and almost laughs, raising his eyebrows to a comical level on his forehead. I realize my eyes are super wide open, and my jaw is slack. I feel my face burn.

Phil looks at Coco and says, "Hey babe, why don't we take this inside?" She giggles as she agrees. My stomach sinks like a stone. What the hell is going on with me? "Oh boy, this is really going to happen," I think to myself. I definitely want to have sex again. This is what I have wanted so much, but I don't have the stomach for it. My courage is fleeing. My anxiety, which was already pretty high, goes skyrocketing as I follow them from the pool area to Coco's little one-bedroom apartment. "Is this really happening?" I think.

Once all three of us walk inside, Coco walks across the room to use the bathroom. Phil pulls me over and starts talking low in my ear. Putting his hand on my shoulder, he gives me the pregame pep talk he knows I desperately need. He whispers the play, and now I know my role and next steps to score. Tonight, I am going to get on the field and get some action. After years of sitting on the sideline, it is my turn.

"OK, here's what's going to happen. I'm going to get her ready for you, so when I call you in, come into the room, and take over." I feel like I am getting ready to bungee jump. Sheer panic sweeps over me. I know from being in the hot tub, Coco is onboard with this. What Phil is doing is setting up or storyboarding the hookup. He will have Coco in position, literally, and all I have to do is walk in and enter in the fun with them. Touchdown! Phil has set up the perfect, no-brainer, 'get into the swing of things' move for me, his down-on-his-luck friend.

As my mind starts racing, Phil picks up Coco caveman style, throws her over his shoulder, and leaves the door open to the bedroom.

Standing in the small living room, I can hear every noise. I start to hear the bed rocking against the wall shortly afterwards, and soft moaning coming from inside. I stand up, my hands sweating like crazy, and my heart feels like it is about to leap out of my chest. It's not from excitement but sheer panic.

I feel like a kid again, like I am required to get up and recite a speech for a public speaking event, but I'm not prepared. The more time goes by, and the longer Phil and Coco are in the bedroom by themselves, the more nervous I get. If I am going to do this thing, I want it to be like ripping off a Band-aid. I just want to get in there and get it over with; I can't stand it any longer.

I walk over to her tiny, white fridge, thinking I might be hungry and some food could calm my nerves. I search around the drawers, find some string cheese, and take a few. I forget that while I can hear every noise Phil and Coco are making, they can also hear every sound I am making outside the bedroom. As I crumple through the string cheese wrappers, the moaning and playful banter stops. Instead, I hear Coco talking in a high-pitched tone.

"Baby, it's nothing," I hear Phil say. Uh oh. Coco says something I can't understand, but I can tell she is not happy.

I then hear footsteps walking briskly. Coco flings the bedroom door wide open and marches angrily toward me.

"What are you doing? Why are you going through my refrigerator?" she asks with frustration, looking up at me with bedhead hair and a furious grimace on her face.

I stammer, "Uh, I was hungry." What the hell have I done? Phil stands there, boxers on, but disheveled, and gives me a wilting look I will never forget.

Coco turns to Phil. "Get him out of here! I feel very uncomfortable with him here," she says as she points to the door. "Leave now!"

My invasion of Coco's fridge is the thread that unravels the entire evening. Not only have I blown my chance to hook up, but I am also ruining Phil's chance too. I realize then that my panic and subsequent snack attack are going to cost Phil his opportunity to finish his fun, too. It should have been a sure thing. And I am completely blowing it.

Silently we walk down the sidewalk from Coco's apartment. Finally, Phil just looks at me and says, "Sheffy, what in the world were you thinking?" And I have no answer. At this moment, I know that Phil realizes that he doesn't even know the depths of my issues. I can see him walking through the scene again in his head, "Man, you're a mess; no one can help you." Phil had set up the T-ball of sex, and I entirely ruined it.

As we continue walking, I am miserable. I want so much to be like Phil. He is my newest role model, in a string of guys that I can never measure up to when it comes to women. And the experience in Coco's apartment makes me realize how many rungs down the ladder from Phil I really am. Just like Phil knows, I know I have issues, but at this moment, it feels like the floor has opened up, and I have fallen even further. I am really discovering my deep dysfunction.

I appreciate what Phil was trying to do. He was trying to provide a spark plug, but what neither of us realized until now is that I need an entire engine overhaul, and one night wasn't going to fix the problem.

AFTER SAYING goodbye to a dear friend in Goose, knowing he was gone for the next 20-plus years in prison, and losing my father forever, I was wide open to welcoming the next disaster into my life. I remember the day when Phil was hired as a personal trainer at our gym. He had a long-braided ponytail, a sleeve of tattoos on his arm, and a few other tattoos on various body parts. I remember thinking, "Who is this dirtbag?" He quickly assimilated with the other trainers, but it took us a while to become friends. Within a few months, a tight group was formed, and a motley crew it was.

Along with Phil and me there was another personal trainer on the team who we called 'Big E,' who was ten years our senior and the most tenured, and Drew, a petite, very cute female who was running the club's nutritional program. That's an interesting part of relationships within the fitness industry. They are very dynamic, ever-changing, and circumstances play a huge role in bringing people together.

At this time, Phil was between places and floating around, staying a night or two with the several lady friends he had at that time. In addition to not having a home, he was driving an older model Hyundai without insurance with an unregistered license plate that an old girlfriend had given him. We drove that car all over the place, and not once were we pulled over. Phil always seemed to be lucky in that way. He would primarily crash at my place over the next several months until he landed a small room in a house in nearby Newport Beach. He shared the place with three sexy Asian girls and one guy, the epitome of a stoner. It was the perfect environment for him. We continued to hang out, but his success with the ladies was the one area in which we did not have anything in common. I desperately wanted to be more like him in that way, but I just didn't have 'IT'. I lacked the confidence and the ability to talk with women in an easy, comfortable way. It was and still is an odd relationship. Phil and I were so very different, but we seemed to both want in some way to be like each other, which is very weird.

Both Phil and Big E were very successful with ladies, and this became even never more apparent when we all took a trip to Palm Springs together. By this time, Drew and Big E were a couple, and Phil was putting the moves on a cute blonde from the gym. And then there was one. I, of course, had no one, but that didn't stop us from going there as a group, albeit with an interesting and lopsided dynamic. I was always the comic relief, which was not the role I wanted, but the humor part was unintentional. I was always a step behind, like I was on the outside, looking in. It was funny and awkward, and that's just where I was during that time.

During the trip, we rented one hotel room. The couples got the beds, of course, and I got a distinguished fifth wheel cot. The room was hot with bodies, and the dry desert air seeping in through the broken seals of the glass door to the balcony left me completely parched. Under cover of darkness, I decided it was safe to grab a large Gatorade bottle from the mini-fridge and loudly chugged until I felt quenched. The silence was broken with laughter from both beds. I couldn't get away with moving a finger on that trip without getting noticed. The group loved me being there, yet I was torn. I felt great that I seemed wanted, but hated that it was at my own expense. That was the last out-of-town group trip I took with them.

There were a few opportunities to earn some respect from Phil. One was with Heather, a cute blonde who was a front desk associate at our gym. She was tan with long legs and was very busty. She was the classic California girl! It started simply enough, but of course, I would complicate it with stupid and awkward behavior. The chance to earn some much needed 'stripes' came one night as we all went out to a local bar for dancing and libations. Phil was a fearless dancer, completely out of sync with the music. He was moving to his own beat, but that didn't stop him from being effective. His nonchalance and coolness were seen as sexy by women. He let the girl be the star and just played it slow, with a 'less is more' attitude. It was genius on his part, and he had this routine down!

As for me, I was riddled by fear early on in the night, but with help from Drew, Big E, and Phil, I had a few drinks, and we hit the dance floor as a group. I did what I had to do and eventually found my way back to my apartment with Heather. I was scared and completely out of my element. This is what I had been pining for, but until this moment had not had the opportunity. Yet, I was full of fear and self-doubt and ultimately unable to follow through. Instead, we spent the night talking and eventually fell asleep. I tried to and wanted to call it a victory, a small success in Craig's very small, rather tiny, black book.

Phil would let me know in no uncertain terms that it was nothing short of failure, however. He was waiting to hear the story. During a break between our morning training sessions, we walked next door to the Coffee Bean. I told him about the night of talking and gentle nothings, and his face turned from promising to utter disgust. In a move that I will never forget, he reached over to my upper sleeve and mimicked pulling stripes off my uniform. It was his way of saying you haven't earned it yet and undeserving of any rank other than a lowly private! It's funny now, and great visual, but at the time it really hurt. I so badly wanted his approval and to be seen as an equal, but I felt I was nowhere near his level. I was set up for success, and I blew a sure thing! I wondered, "Is there any hope for me?"

A few weeks later, after things with Heather cooled off, I had lost the little bit of confidence I had left. Seeing my dismay, Phil invited me out with him and a personal training client named Coco. It went horribly and another SURE THING was blown!

After this debacle, I wanted to make amends. I embarked on a seemingly harmless local outing with the whole group. We took a trip across the street for happy hour after our Friday afternoon personal training sessions, which eventually became a ritual. Again, I was alone with the two other couples. On our way to the bar, there was a large highway with a tall concrete median that we needed to cross. Each couple took a turn and sprinted across the first set of three lanes to the median, where each guy would lift his lady up and over, and then they would run across the second set of lanes. It came to my turn. As the last one, I sprinted with all my might, trying to ramp up enough speed to hurl myself up and over the median. My shorter leg length didn't leave a lot of room for error. I quickly found myself sprawled, open-legged, across the concrete median. Cars began whizzing by on both sides. All I heard was hoots and hollers coming from my friends. I finally detangled myself and sprinted over to the other side to join them. "That was the funniest thing I have ever seen!!" they all said in almost unison. Tears were streaming from their faces. My enjoyment of being the entertainment faded in that moment, and again, I knew it was time for a change. I was the loveable loser who had grown weary of my role.

As I looked for that next step or sign from the universe, hoping that one day I would be normal, I thought about what might have been if only I had made some different decisions early on. What would have happened if I had taken advantage of all the opportunities that presented themselves? I had been an angry kid, a scared kid, and someone who put up so many walls that I had blinded myself to the 'what-ifs' in life, and was only capable of looking at the empty glass in front of me.

SESSION 9: SUNSET BOULEVARD

I look around nervously at home, waiting for Sara to pick me up. Trying to stand upright, I want to look normal, in the way that drunk guys try to look casual, and give off the 'I'm just standing here being sober' vibe.

Sara is different. With other girls, I have to suffer through the 'chatty' part of dates. I don't want to hear about their model/actress vision garbage. To make it through the ridiculous small talk, I resort to drinking alcohol (which I normally avoid) just to dull my senses enough to sit there and take it.

But with Sara, we skipped right through the small talk. She took the wheel, and I'm happy to be in the passenger seat and ride shotgun. Before I know it, we are spending a lot of time together, eating out, going to the movies, and exercising.

It's going well. It's too good. Two months in, and I panic. "What the hell?" I think to myself. Things are going well, but I am afraid. I haven't yet read the 'next chapter in my relationship' dating manual and have no skills in my toolbox to cope with this intermediate-level dating game.

Picking up the Jägermeister bottle before our movie date, I take sip after sip. It is nasty. I'm not really a drinker, so I start picking up the pace, concerned that I'm not feeling the effects of the alcohol. Until suddenly, all of the drinks hit me at once. Jägermeister is powerful, and I am severely buzzed.

Sara comes driving up to my apartment complex, and I get in her car. She smiles at me but turns her attention back to the road and continues driving.

We drive to the theater on the busy Santa Monica promenade, and she starts driving up the many levels of the parking garage in a series of circles. With all the tight circles she is making, I feel awful, and start making noises. "What's wrong with you," she asks, and then her face slowly dissolves. She immediately notices I am buzzed. "Oh my God," she says, looking both ways as if praying no one sees my condition. "Really, Craig?" I motion toward the theater, and she shakes her head.

"No way. I'm taking you home."

On the ride back to my place, she is stonily silent.

It is the beginning of the end. I knew I wasn't equipped to handle a healthy relationship, and so I throw a huge Jägermeister-shaped wrench into the works. And with that, I sink our ship.

AFTER A FEW MORE ATTEMPTS WITH the female population, and enduring a now stagnant personal training role in Orange County, I kept failing miserably. I decided to move north to the mecca of fitness at the time, Los Angeles. This was a common theme for me; make a mess of things and move away. My fellow trainers and quasi-mentors, Phil and Big E, tried to convince me not to leave, saying that LA was a dump, not the place I thought it was, and that ultimately, it was not going to make me happy.

I didn't listen, which was uncharacteristic for me at that time. I was still very much under the spell of both Phil and Big E, and usually followed their lead. However, I ignored their advice, packed up and took two buses and a train, and arrived at Union Station in downtown LA, late on a Sunday. With $350 in cash and a large duffel bag with everything I owned, I took the Big Blue Bus to a hostel in Santa Monica about two blocks from the beach. The room had eight bunk beds, and down the hall was a communal bathroom. Almost all of the other residents were travelers, there to sightsee. Many were from other countries that wanted to see famous LA sites and Hollywood.

I was on a completely different path. I only had enough money to live at the hostel and eat for about 30 days. Luckily, I found cheap eats and existed on 99 cent donuts and the dollar menu from Burger King. I came to love that dollar menu. A lucky find for me was a local hotel with a happy hour buffet. For the cost of one drink, you could eat all you wanted. It wasn't a happy hour for me; however, it was a necessity. I made it work and was grateful. I rode the city buses everywhere around. After about a week, I felt compelled to call America's Top Ten Most Wanted hotline and tell them I had found everyone. Nevertheless, my transportation served its purpose.

I still did not have much money, but upgraded slightly to a small shared house in Venice Beach, a few blocks from the site of the original Gold's Gym on Pacific Avenue. I could only afford a small spot on the floor. They literally rented out space, in addition to rooms, depending on how much you paid. It was a great location. It was also near the very popular Gold's Gym on Hampton Drive, where I spent a lot of time. It was as active and colorful as you could imagine. Actors, bodybuilders, models; everyone was in there. A few weeks in, I joined a group from the gym and walked to a nearby Koo-Koo-Roos, a popular grilled chicken place, for a post-workout meal with actor James Caan. I really didn't know this at the time, but that kind of experience was the norm there. Everybody just blended in, and exercise was the common ground.

I continued to spend my days riding the bus to local gyms that I found in the yellow pages. I would get on and off the bus for the next several days, and after visiting over twenty gyms, I landed an entry-level personal training position at a boutique fitness chain in Santa Monica called Bodies in Motion. At the time, they were trying to implement an in-house training program. Up until that point, they only hired independent trainers, and they were very good ones. Several were former professional athletes and accomplished fitness professionals. I was in the right place at the right time. They offered a modest salary as opposed to paying by session. This was better for me, as I desperately needed a consistent income.

I loved being in LA, and like a vast majority of people who move out there, I also got the itch to be an actor. Luck would shine my way as one of my very first personal training clients at the gym was a talent manager with a large entertainment agency. She pointed me in the right direction. "I totally get you, Craig," Ellen said. "You've got to get involved in classes. That is how you make it out here," she said with conviction. "Thanks, Ellen," I said to her and quickly joined an acting class in Hollywood and an improv theater class in Santa Monica. I kept a solid presence at the gym, doing a split schedule, and would take acting classes in the middle of the day and on weekends. I really wanted to be an actor, to become famous, and felt during this time that anything less would mean I was a failure. I started performing at open mics in local comedy clubs, practicing what I had learned in improv. I loved it. The adrenaline was intense and made me feel alive again, full of purpose and worth.

I was around some very talented trainers during this time. I also interacted with many people, in addition to James Caan and Ellen, in the entertainment industry who were members. On one of my days off, I walked into the World Gym in Venice Beach. At the front desk was a white-haired man sitting very comfortably, like he owned the place. Actually, he did!

"Are you Joe Gold?" I asked him. He said yes, and I couldn't believe it! I spent an entire hour talking with Joe, the man who founded Gold's Gym. It was one of those fantastic moments living in Los Angeles that I will never forget. I reminisced about my time with Gold's Gym on the East Coast, and I felt connected. It resonates still with me to have had an opportunity to share my experiences with him about being a part of the growth of the fitness enterprise he had founded, so many years before.

I soon found a small studio apartment several blocks from the gym in Santa Monica, and I was living on my own, feeling a sense of independence. I continued on this path when I met Sara. She was a member of the gym and quickly took a liking to me. I would like to say it was me, but I think I just happened to be in the right place at the right time. This was a new theme I had never experienced. She was a nanny to Steven Spielberg's kids and lived in his pool house a few miles from the gym in Pacific Palisades. I started as her personal trainer, but we were soon spending a great deal of time together, eating out and going to the movies, exercising together, and acting like normal young adults in a relationship.

It was all going pretty well until about 2 months in. We had planned to see a movie at the nearby theater, and I beforehand drank several small mini bottles of Jägermeister. I was not a drinker by any means and never really took a liking to the taste of alcohol. I did, however, use it from time to time, usually before a date or any interaction with a woman. I liked muting the sabotaging thoughts that often crept into my head. Alcohol gave me the ability to filter out the noise and only focus on what I needed to hear. This helped me stay in a positive place with these women, rather than ranting or leading the conversation to a dark or uncomfortable place. But this time, I overdid it.

Looking back, I really didn't need to do that. All I had to was stay present and have fun, but I couldn't do it. For me being around women wasn't fun!

Soon after that incident, Sara and I went to a small party at Albert's home. Albert was another trainer at the gym and would eventually become the Assistant Fitness Manager. His cousin, Patrick, was there as well, and we all enjoyed a nice evening. I was oblivious to anything outside of myself, and my new-found infatuation with Sara. A few days later, while Sara and I were having dinner at the Cheesecake Factory, her phone rang. She quickly looked at the number and turned the phone over. Curious, I asked who it was. She answered very casually, "Patrick." "Interesting," I thought. "So, why is Patrick calling you?" I asked. No words came out of her mouth, but her eyes quickly told me, 'Because I'm into him, Craig.' She tried so hard not to meet my eyes.

I had been scouting acting workshops all over the country and had found one in which I was interested. I secured a spot and left a week later for a 3-week intensive acting workshop in New York City. I left LA with a horrible taste in my mouth. I loved the workshop and was feeling more confident in being in front of people. I had started to embrace my humor, although it would be years until I finally saw it as a gift.

While in New York City, I would walk the streets at night after the class and visit local comedy clubs. I'd sip soda water with lime and enjoyed seeing everyone get up and just rant about their lives. It was raw, sometimes not funny at all, but that made it even more amusing for me. I felt envious of the comedians. I craved that space, that freedom I saw in their sets.

I then returned to LA after finishing the 3-week workshop, but could not get past the discomfort of this latest relationship failure with Sara. I felt embarrassed, and I was isolated now from the very gym at which I worked. Patrick's cousin was my boss, and enduring the thought of seeing Sara come to exercise was unbearable. I now had nothing left holding me in California. My family had dispersed, my brother and sister were rarely around or seeking an audience with me, and this last relationship left me disappointed, yet again. I chose to leave and start again. I look back now and wonder why I couldn't just get over it. Rather than deal maturely with the situation and own responsibility, I decided again to run. I would now be heading to the Big Apple!

SESSION 10: CAN'T BUY ME LOVE

There aren't a lot of rules in a sex dungeon. When she invites me over, I sit obediently, awaiting orders from Mistress Jada. One of her favorite activities is to start our rendezvous by leaving me to wait. It seems to increase her excitement, and I am happy to oblige. I sit there wondering, does she play the same dynamic with her actual clients? Or, as one of her non-paying hookups who allowed her to have sex free of stress, commitment, and drama, do I get different treatment?

She called me up earlier today.

"Craig, I'll be done at 9 tonight. I want you at the dungeon at 8, so you can watch me with my last client."

I come over, anticipating another all night, non-stop session, and I'm excited to see her in action and in her element finally. When I arrive, I gaze around the room. Huge mirrors reflect my face as I soak in my surroundings. As soon as I walk in, I step over big dog chains. There is a dog bowl on the floor and cages large enough for a person. From the ceiling, there are suspension rings and chains. It looks like a medieval torture chamber. Leather masks, chains, and whips are everywhere. There are armless chairs so the girls can straddle their clients.

I see her in the corner. Pulling her thigh highs up her legs and snapping them in place, she looks up. She points firmly to a stool a few feet from her side. I quickly obey. From my seat, I see another man enter the room. He looks like he came straight from the Wall Street trading floor in his expensive suit. He doesn't care that I am there. I certainly don't care.

After Mr. Wall Street pays his tribute fee to Miss Jada, she summarily dismisses him. Almost an hour has passed, and I am ready to get my time in with Mistress Jada and embark on all the new ideas springing to life in my head after what I had just witnessed.

"Want to go to the movies?" I know what she's really asking, and I agree. We buy our tickets, walk into the back row of the theater, and have sex six ways to Sunday right there in the open.

I reminisce to myself; I think about Sara and realize she has nothing on Jada. If Sara was like being at the helm of a sailboat, this lady like is pedal to the metal on a speedboat. She dictates everything about sex; "Do this, sit there, pull harder!" And if for any reason there is doubt about Jada's commitment to this lifestyle, she has the word SLUT tattooed on her ass in red.

On our way back from the theater, I lean in and say to her, "Man, I really missed you."

In the middle of the street, she spins around on her heels and looks harshly at me. Damn, I know I slipped up.

"Look, Craig, this isn't about me liking you or you liking me. This is about sex for sport. This is about me f*cking you."

I stand corrected.

I WAS in a funk moving back to New York City. I had yet to have any relationship last longer than a month or two. Frustrated with my inability to understand relationships, I ventured through more precarious avenues where the expectations weren't as high.

In the early 2000s, not everyone had personal computers the way we do today. There were large internet cafes in New York where sex workers would buy time on the internet and place ads. I would go online all the time. Soon I discovered many of them were located only a block or two away from me at any given time. I was in the best locale to capitalize on this situation, as being a block away from Times Square gave me access to an unimaginable volume of women.

In an online chat room one night, I came across the handle, 'thenefariousone', for a very sexy blond Asian woman. After some fun banter and saucy discourse, we quickly moved from chatting online to meeting in person. At the time, she was working as a dominatrix at a BDSM dungeon on West 36th Street. She was in a 3rd-floor loft in a very discreet building. By this time, I was completely dysfunctional when it came to relationships and interacting with women. This particular interaction was as simple as they come. All 'thenefariousone' wanted to do was have sex as wildly and intensely as possible, then rest and repeat. She wore fishnet thigh highs, black wristlets that resembled a dark and evil wonder woman, and had 'SLUT' tattooed across her backside. She answered the door in her five-inch high heels, a black leather whip in hand, and two bleach-blonde pigtails in her hair. There was no cuddling, no dates, no kind words. It was real and raw!

Over the next days, I learned that she loved danger and was sexually fearless. We'd often meet in a movie theater or other public places to test the limits without getting caught. I would often spend time at the dungeon and watch the parade of professionals, husbands, fathers, and businessmen go in and out to fulfill the fantasies they couldn't share with their wives or partners. Though there was an authentic aspect to this dalliance, it didn't last long. It's probably not intended to last. It did, however, set the 'sex for sport bar' to a level that would be very hard to find in the girl next door. This woman, Jada, lived in the sex world. When not fulfilling her job duties as a dominatrix, she was holding her own sport sex sessions with friends from the porn industry, in front of and behind the camera, anything goes! In fact, she called me to cancel our next scheduled meeting because her undercarriage was so sore that she needed more time to heal after one of her sex sessions. Wow, this was some crazy news to consider.

One time, she came to my apartment, and we were in the bedroom for 8 to 9 hours. By the time she walked out, my bedroom had looked like we were testing missiles.

Jada lived and breathed this world. She didn't go home to a boyfriend. All of her friends were in the adult film and BDSM industry. Being Mistress Jada was a part of her alter ego. What she provided was immediate gratification to the 10th degree. I didn't have to work for sex, and there were no rules. With her, it was just 0 to 60 all of the time. That girl did things that would scare Stephen King.

This flipped my arousal template on its head. After you have experienced that kind of thrill ride, you don't have the patience for hanging out with 'vanilla' girls. I had achieved the highest level of sexual evolution.

She was in the upper echelon of sex for sport, and no one had come close to her level of physicality and thirst for being dominated and dishing it back out. Though I always wanted more and more, it probably would have taken me to a place of no return had our time together lasted longer. I certainly wasn't looking out for my safety. Things ended organically with Jada. There were fewer calls, and we moved farther and farther apart. I can only assume someone else caught her eye.

I once saw a t-shirt that read, 'For every super-hot chick, there is someone else out there who is bored with her.' This notion became somewhat of a mantra for me over the next few years.

My time with Jada showed me the darker side of the sex industry, and just like drugs or alcohol, it can be just as addictive and dangerous. I am glad I made it out alive.

I quickly moved to a fitness director position and returned to the Gold's Gym organization. That was when I really took 'sex for sport' to a whole new level. I was unhappy and didn't know how to deal with it. I was acting out and expressing myself in the only way I really knew how. Every day, I was leaving work and lining up an ensemble of hookers who were currently in the rotation. Some nights they weren't available, and I had to start from scratch by scouring the internet, making calls, and setting up the meets. Many times, the planning would take the entire evening, but I was committed, and I felt I couldn't do without.

There were nights I was resigned to in-call services, meaning I had to go to the hookers. This is always a dangerous proposition as you never really know what you are walking into. By the time I found out, often I was already vulnerable. There were a few close calls, and the odds were continuously stacking up against me, but by now, I was compelled to keep doing it. It wasn't for the danger, or some sick and twisted thrill of wanting to get caught secretly. It was a deep-rooted, tangible need. These compulsions were the seeds of my self-destruction.

This went on for almost 2 years. All-consuming, my desires rendered me useless to the women who were looking for normal, balanced relationships. This was self-destruction at its finest, and I was loose in uncharted territory. I became less and less invested in my work. After initially getting off to a very solid start, both financially and operationally, I would never fully resume the 'A game' work ethic and results driven attitude that I had earlier on in my career.

Tremendous turbulence and internal rifts were emerging within the company at this time, too. The gym was owned by one man, 'G,' who was a very smart businessman. He had supposedly worked as a doorman at the famous Studio 54 during its heyday. He was a chiropractor that made the transition into owning and operating a full service fitness facility. After initially practicing as a chiropractic doctor, he made the career leap to health and fitness. He had a deep-rooted entrepreneurial spirit and built this gym one room at a time. There were two primary sales stars, Max and Dennis, who had been there for several years and were itching for an ownership role.

Max and Dennis made their move to leave, and G offered them a stake in the business. The two would eventually buy the business from G. They had a contract to pay out a note over a certain period of time. It quickly got ugly, and egos got in the way. G quickly real-

ized that he didn't like being behind the scenes and feeling insignif-
icant, so the fighting began, and everyone became a victim. The
environment was heavy and divided into two camps, the G camp
and the M and D camp. I was smack in the middle. I felt no fulfillment at work and was acting out every night. I wish I had been
mature enough to be a better team player, a better leader. Instead I
just stood by and did nothing.

The less I did at work during the day, the more I did at night. By
this time, a lot of the hookers on the internet were college girls, and
some were women with actual jobs who wanted extra money. Even
so, I could never be sure who would show up. So, I devised a
routine where I would ask the women to meet on the corner of 59th
and 7th Avenue. I had rented an apartment from a personal
training client along Central Park South. I was finally confident and
felt like I was in control of my sexual prowess, owning every move,
action, and choice. I could see this corner perfectly from my apartment. I would use a pair of high-powered binoculars while laying
flat on my stomach on my balcony to get a better, surreptitious
look. The suspense made the entire process much more fulfilling
for me. After I got a good look at my arriving 'guest,' I would give
the red or green light call to them. This process took almost 3 hours
every night, just in prep time alone.

I was a good host; I would offer the women wine and would
often run a bath for them to enjoy themselves. It gave me a feeling
that I had a normal relationship, but it was nothing even remotely
close to that. I kept this up until I literally ran out of money and no
longer could endure the days at work anymore. I suspect I spent
over $50,000 over 14 months, but the cost to my mental health and
self-esteem was much more. I made myself, an already dysfunctional person, even worse in the areas of relationships and sexual
intimacy. Even the times I would go out on actual dates, I always
had an after-dinner nightcap 'sure thing' on speed dial, accessible
to me, into the late hours of the night. It was the only way I could
function around women. I would continue to utilize alcohol in
small, carefully timed and metered amounts to just get through

dates without showing any discomfort and lack of patience. I just wasn't open or wanting to put in the effort, yet.

Around that time, I thought again about Andréa, the girl I met at my grandma's condo when I was a teenager. She entered my thoughts one day, so I searched the internet for her, and found her email. We emailed some small talk, and soon after she mentioned she'd be in the city to attend a conference at Columbia University, I was still working at Gold's Gym in Manhattan. We met at a restaurant inside of Penn Station and talked for hours. There was literally no one else in this area of the restaurant, just the two of us, no friend to interrupt or whisk me away this time. She did most of the talking, and spoke about her life and marriage, showed me pictures, and she seemed to be in a good place.

However, there were cracks in her marriage and they began to get larger, as she spoke of them more often. In phone conversations after we met, she shared her suspicions that her cop husband was leading a double life. During this period, a door opened, and she became 'accessible' to me for the first time since that first meeting at the pool in the Hemispheres, over 1,500 miles away and 20 years ago.

Having grown impatient from having to take a backseat all those years ago, this time I pushed. I was hoping to swoop her up and have a real relationship, ignoring reality and what should have been visible dysfunction; there was something familiar and straightforward about her that attracted me. We continued to spend time together, and after dinner one night, we returned to my place in midtown Manhattan. This time there would be no interruptions, no other plans.

Looking back, we were there for two very different reasons. She was lost and seeking connection and comfort, but I was just trying to recapture a teenage crush. It was novel, but it didn't last, and under those circumstances, how could it? That was the first and last sexual experience we would have. Nothing was right about us at this time, and there wasn't a future going forward. She was still very consumed with her life on Long Island, and she was an adult. I was still a teenager in a lot of ways. Looking back, I wish I had put aside my childish infatuation and been a better friend to her.

A few months went by, and then Andréa showed up at a comedy club I was performing at in New York City. After the show, she confided in me that her suspicions about her husband's double life were indeed true. He was involved in a homosexual relationship with a fellow officer on the police force. Of course, I couldn't resist and I pressed her again for more, hoping this recent development in her marriage would have changed things. But this time she was more direct and told me she wasn't interested in pursuing a relationship. I took it like a teenager and pouted, but eventually let it go, and that was it. She has since found love, started a family, and still resides on Long Island. I am happy for her and like to remember that special day by the pool. To me, she will always be that cute girl in the striped bikini, and now that's enough for me.

SESSION 11: FINDING GRACE

Day after day, she keeps talking about it.

"Enough, Marissa! Leave me alone about this already," I say.

"C'mon, Craig! You've got to try it. You will love hot yoga! Please, come with me just once. If you hate it, I promise I won't bug you anymore," Marissa, a member that I often chat with at the gym, said. She just keeps hounding me. She is absolutely relentless!

I'm feeling more agreeable than usual today, having come off a good set the night before at the comedy club, so I relent.

"OK, fine! I'll go...if it will get you off my back!" Marissa is happy; I am skeptical.

We walk to the Bikram Yoga Studio on 8th Avenue. I shuffle my feet as Marissa almost skips to the studio. I'm already annoyed, and as soon as we walk in, I break out in a sweat. I am about to turn and complain to Marissa when I see her.

She is facing towards the front of the class, anticipating the session to begin. Her name is Grace. She is sexy but in a confident way, in a 'not-trying-too-hard' way. While she's fit, she has a lovely curvy body. The air, which is already in the 100 degree range, starts to feel even hotter to me.

For months, I frequent the class as often as I can. She and I say a little 'hello' here, a little 'hi' there, but that's it. One day after class, on a whim, I walk up to her.

"Um, hi, Grace."

She smiles back and says hi.

"Would you like to grab a drink?" I am drenched with sweat, and a little knot of fear tightens in my gut. Will she say yes?

"Sure," she says, still smiling. I'm surprised and scared at the same time.

Walking down the street together, we talk a little, when suddenly the thought crosses my mind like a breaking news banner. YOU ONLY HAVE $20! Oh no! I live only a few blocks from the yoga studio, and it's common for me not to bring a wallet, just a few bucks, or sometimes no money.

I try really hard to look like everything is normal as we walk to a nearby bar.

"Do you want to sit outside?" she asks. "Sure," I say, pulling up a chair.

We sit outside on the sidewalk table, and as if it was scripted, some fellow yogis walk by, smiling at both of us; I'm riding off the wave of confidence, feeling that these mutual friends are approving of us sitting together. I'm pumped. By the time we order a drink, five mutual acquaintances have passed and say hello. I think to myself, "I'm in, she thinks I'm cool, these people we both know are the validation I needed!"

I'm now partway through my first drink, and I'm not freaking out! She is leaning towards me, listening to what I have to say.

"I've started doing stand-up at some clubs in town," I share. Who is this talking, I think to myself. I don't do small talk! But I do now; I'm small talking! And she's listening!

"Wow, that's amazing!" she says, seemingly in awe. "How do you have the courage to stand up on stage and do that?"

I answer with an air of confidence. It is a fantastic feeling; emotions are creeping up that I have never felt before. I'm not forcing it at all. In fact, our conversation is effortless, and I am feeling great.

"Would you like another drink?" I ask.

What am I thinking? I have NO money on me! Oh shit. Time to confess.

"Um, can I borrow $20?" I blush and stammer, completely embarrassed.

Giggling, she says, "Of course!" She is so sweet.

I WAS STILL WORKING at Gold's Gym in New York City but now only as a personal trainer, as I was no longer a member of the management team. I moved into a small studio apartment near the Port Authority Bus Terminal.

I had also started performing standup a few times a week and was feeling a little more confident as a person and professional during this time. Working in the heart of the NYC health and fitness scene in the theater district, I also found my time being spent surrounded by a lot of gay men.

"Hey, Craig! Looking good today!" Nicholas yelled across the gym. I had a great rapport with him and his friends; they all loved pumping me up with compliments when I would workout. "Hey Studly!" they would say as I held a barbell across my shoulders. I could see myself in the mirror turning red, with a slight glint of laughter on the corners on my lips. It was so hard to stay serious, hearing how invested they were in providing words of encouragement.

My gay friends were pivotal in helping me get a better sense of who I was. Much more helpful than most of the straight guys I'd come across, I learned a lot about culture through our conversations at the gym. More than that, these guys, many of whom were part of the entertainment and fashion industries, taught me about sensitivity in a way my mother never had.

Up until that point, I'd had a life filled with empty and selfish relationships. I imagine some of these gay men found me attractive on some level, but that wasn't the basis of our relationship, as we were actively non-judgmental of one another. We could talk for hours, and I'd share perspectives from a harsh lens. They offered solace to those years of pain, speaking with compassion. "Craig, that's terrible about Goose," Ricky would repeat. "I'm sure you will be friends again one day. He'll see that you did what was right," he tried to assure me. My stories offered intrigue and scandal from a straight man's perspective. I provided what I could to those relationships, while always making sure we kept our boundaries in full view. I grew to enjoy those conversations and the ability to share openly without fear of repercussions or judgement. Even if they were judging me, they never showed it openly or callously.

My gay friends taught me things like the difference between a handsome and ugly penis. They helped me identify with my sexuality and my feminine side. Being empathetic, I would always embrace them and even kiss them on the cheek. I joked, "Unless you're bigger than me, I'm OK with this." I felt I could be myself with them the way I couldn't be with a woman.

It was about acceptance and a sense of love for people. I wanted acceptance, and they wanted acceptance. For these friendships, I didn't see the penis and vagina. We were all friends because we genuinely cared about each other.

What I also soon found out is that there is nothing more attractive to a woman than a man who is so secure in his masculinity that he can be friends with gay guys, or at least that's how it was in NYC. A lot of straight guys have a tough time straddling that wall.

There was a girl in the gym who was hounding me to try hot yoga. Day after day, she kept talking about it, until one day I finally went. Without her being annoying and relentless, I would have never met my wife; I will always be grateful to Marissa.

That's when I saw Grace. A beautiful, vibrant, Asian goddess. She had a slim yet curvy physique and a smile that reached across the room. Her long brown hair seemed to sweep like silk across her back. I made eye contact and immediately felt my cheeks get red hot. Her brown, almond-shaped eyes were peering back at me with a sensual "hello" whispering to me.

One day after the class, I composed myself and approached her.

"Um, hi Grace," I muttered. "Hey, Craig, " she said. "How did you like the class?" she asked as we stepped into the elevator together. "It was incredible. I wish I were as flexible as you," I said quickly. She giggled softly and shifted her weight back and forth. "Would you like to go out for a drink?" I asked, filled with confidence, considering she would probably say no. "Sure!" she exclaimed.

When Grace and I went to an outside bar, mutual gay acquaintances of ours from the yoga studio passed by and said hello. The fact that I have no hang-ups about gay people was attractive to Grace.

This is the day that Grace, without hesitation, helped me out with the check when I didn't have enough cash with me. When I asked her out, I sincerely thought to myself; she'll never say yes to me. So with only $20 in my pocket, we strolled to the outside seating area of the local bar. The breeze would pick up from time to time. I sat there, watching her mouth move up and down, mesmerized by her words, the sound of her voice, and the way I got a warm rush of emotion each time she made eye contact and smiled. "So, did you want to have another drink?" I asked, hoping she'd say no. "Yeah, that would be great," she said enthusiastically. She was obviously enjoying the conversation and company from her body language. She leaned into the table as she continued with her story.

"I'm originally from Montana, but fell in love with New York. I am a flight attendant and have always loved my layovers here. I decided to move out here and asked for a transfer to be based out here instead," she explained. "My mom came out here with me when I moved. She lives on the Upper East Side," she told me. I was intrigued by her sense of independence, and yet through the strength, I saw femininity and vulnerability that I had never seen in combination before. She felt like one of the guys, spoke like a woman with high intelligence, and yet, was the sexiest woman I'd ever had sitting in front of me, holding every level of my interest and engagement.

"Is everything okay?" she asked. I had little sweat droplets forming on my forehead. Slowly I had been formulating in my mind how to tell her that I only had a $20 bill in my pocket. "Um, can I borrow 20 dollars?" I barely managed to get out.

Grace let out an amazing laugh. "Of course," she giggled. "Craig, no sweat. I've got this," she said, calmly and confidently. Still, to this day, she never forgets that story and is more than happy to tell anyone who will listen. She gets incredible enjoyment from poking fun at me for that.

We began an interesting friendship. Grace was unlike any other woman I had met in my life. She was sexy, not just 'I want to get in your pants' sexy, but sexy in every way. Her face would always light up with this gorgeous smile when I came into the room. Her hair swept around her face, leaving me enchanted in a way I still can't explain.

As our friendship evolved, Grace and I would go to parties hosted by her flight attendant friends. There would be seventy-eight gay guys, two women, and me. This community resembled a sorority of sorts, with one exception. At a party with these gay men, they wouldn't have any food. Most of the gay men in this group didn't want to have a lot of food because they were afraid of getting heavy. Also, they expressed a high level of dissatisfaction at watching other men eat. These men were more about alcohol. I would attend the parties and say to Grace, "They know I'm coming. I'm okay with being ogled, but only if we can order some pizza." I felt similar to how I imagine a girl with big boobs at a construction site must feel.

Grace challenged me with confidence, not from an arrogant selfishness, but in a loving, endearing way that made me melt when I was with her. We had lots of early ups and downs, never actually 'committing' to having a dedicated relationship until about 2005.

Before that could happen, I hit a low point and lost momentum in NYC. I left for several months, staying in Laguna Beach with my sister. I had gone from being a fitness director at a club in Times Square to walking around in the same yoga clothes every damn day. I really was doing nothing except yoga, watching TV, and probably running away. One day, carrying my sun-faded gym tote, I bumped into a gentleman who motioned to me.

"Hey," he said, "There's a food truck for us!"

I suddenly realized he was pointing to a food truck that provided meals for the homeless. Looking at my ratty attire and bag, I could see why the guy was mistaken.

"He thinks I'm homeless," I thought to myself. I wasn't far from it; I had no apartment, no prospects, and barely any money. I looked at the food truck and answered, "Well, I am hungry. I could have a little nosh right now."

Nevertheless, during this time, I kept in touch with Grace. When it came time to decide to stay in California or head back to New York, she was the only reason I moved back. No more running. I was compelled to see her again, to find a way to be in her life. Thoughts rushed against me. "What are you doing? You have no money, no apartment, nothing there," my mind would yell at me. But this time, there was something stronger than that internal voice. Reconciling this internal rift was something I would have to put on hold, as I found my way back to Grace.

I started renting a small office space in Tribeca and turned it into an efficiency apartment. I was showering at the gym and using a small office kitchenette for running water. It wasn't ideal, but it served my purposes.

Grace and I were spending more and more time together, and she was a real source of comfort and support. She would meet me near the gym where I was working and have coffee during my breaks. We would do this for another 2 months.

One day we met at a local Starbucks, and she asked, "Where are you living? You haven't invited me to your place since you got back to the city." Ashamed, I said, "I'm just embarrassed, Grace." I continued, "I'm renting a small office in Tribeca, and it doesn't have running water. It would be tough to have you visit." She looked at me, and without hesitation, she asked: "Will you move in with me?" I replied in a bit of shock. "Really? Are you sure?" I questioned, with worry that I would let her down in some way. I knew immediately that she was opening her home to me and that this was the biggest thing that had ever been offered to me by someone in my life. I sat thinking, "She doesn't see me as a charity case; she sees me as a partner."

Finally I met my match. I knew I would never find someone who lit me up like Grace. Her energy engulfed me. Her spirit, her ability to stand up for what she wanted, and at the very same moment, show openness and feminine strength were like nothing I'd ever encountered.

She had a studio apartment in Forest Hills, Queens. I moved in 2 weeks after our conversation at Starbucks; I even left the futon and my TV behind and just packed up my clothing. She met me at the office space and helped me move those items onto the sidewalk for trash pickup. As we drove away in her small Honda Civic, I looked back on a life of empty possessions and felt hopeful. This was the first new start that I was running toward, and with intention.

We lived in harmony for several months, where we grew in love, friendship, and emotions that I came to embrace. One night, as we were heading up to the apartment, we stepped onto the elevator. Our hands brushed against one another, and it sent a shot of electricity through my arm. I turned and looked at her, her eyes only a few inches lower than my own. I stared at her face and said, "We should get married." After a quick second, she said, "OK." That was it. I took her and kissed her, smiling from ear to ear. We were engaged. No-fuss, no extra added romance, just the way she had always been. Grace and I were married one year later in Las Vegas with only two other people there.

She wore a beautiful brown dress that I picked out. I look back on that moment of saying "I do" and know I will cherish it forever. We returned home, and it was back to work. We had a great time living together in Queens, and for the first time in my life, I really felt comfortable and knew what home was.

SESSION 12: GRACE UNDER PRESSURE

What the hell am I doing? What have I done? In the previous 5 months, I stayed away from home, away from Grace. I just despise myself. Looking in the mirror is torture. I hate the man I see. He is a wreck, an asshole.

From the rundown, roach-infested hotel in Midtown East Manhattan, I have been calling for sex workers over and over. On this night, I just can't even do that. My pants are hanging on my hips, evidence that I am literally wasting away. Even the thought of another sex binge isn't doing it for me. Though I have been with woman after woman, I still feel this gaping hole in my soul that no amount of human contact can fill.

Wanting quiet, not able to channel the chatter in my brain, I walk outside of the hotel. Circling the block, over and over, I start to disassociate from my body. Lacking in sleep and barely able to stomach food, I have lost almost 40 pounds over the last several weeks. For the next 2 hours, I just keep walking around the hotel.

Why am I here? I think to myself with every lap; I'm so worthless, I'm such a loser. With every step I take, with every thought I tell myself, I spiral down further into anxiety, unhappiness, and hopelessness. The negativity in my brain, which has not slept in over three days, is getting louder and more insistent. The urge to make all the pain stop grows stronger.

Close to 5 am, I hatch a plan. I will sprint in front of the next speeding bus and end it all.

"On the next lap, I will find the bus," I say to myself, feverishly. "Right out on the corner of Lexington," I tell myself over and over that this is it. There is no other way out. I have nothing, and I have alienated everyone in my life. All the people in my life – my mom, my dad, the teachers in school, the principal, my fellow fitness colleagues – are right. I am worthless, I am a loser, and I am the lowest of the low. I am going to end it.

The moment of truth comes as I turn onto Lexington Avenue. With no energy at all, I crumple into a heap on the steps of a nearby townhome. Staring at the passing bus, I feel nothing. On this cold September night, wearing a thin cotton t-shirt and jeans, I should be shivering, but I feel nothing. I am spent.

All I can think in this moment is, I have to call Grace. It is a ridiculous thought; she has every reason not to help me, and I have no right to ask for help in the first place.

My hands tremble as I dial her number from my cell phone. Please be there, I think.

"Craig?!" she says. She answers. SHE ANSWERS! My hands are shaking, but I keep talking.

"Please help me. I'm sorr –"

"Where are you?" she says as she cuts me off. "Where are you?!" I tell her my location, and in 15 minutes, she pulls up near the curb where I am slumped on the ground.

She arrives at that doorstep with open arms. As she puts her arms around me and helps me stand up, I can't look her in the eyes. I melt into the seat of the car as she helps me into the passenger side door.

When I wake up at our house, Grace is holding my head.

"Hey baby," she says, with a small smile. "Here, have some of this."

As she helps me raise my head, I gently drink the coconut water she offers to me. She wants me to live. She wants ME. After I acted the way I did, after I ran away and hurt her horribly, she still loves me.

I was extremely unhappy at work. And I was caught up in it, resulting first in my not going onstage as often, and then not at all. When I wasn't on stage, I really felt it. I wasn't doing what I was supposed to be doing. There is a saying when a guy isn't happy in his heart and mind, he gets happy with his penis.

That's what happened to me. When I got caught up at work, the negative thoughts were lying in wait for me. They came back. "You're nothing! You're no good!" These thoughts dominated my mind.

I have no coping skills. I went back to sex binging. I thought if I could have sex every day, I could make the pain go away. I tried to fill the hole in my soul with sex.

It had nothing to do with Grace. She and I were getting along well. It is all about me not being able to make the changes in my life. Grace is always supportive. It isn't so much that I pushed her away as it was that I started running to escape myself.

Grace is collateral damage because, at this point in my life, I cannot exist in my own skin. I want to run away from myself, and unfortunately, that happens to include Grace. I feel so horrible about myself and have so little self-worth. I am completely in my own head. It is as if I keep filling a garbage disposal with shit, but I never press the button to clear it. Even with 6 1/2 years of being married, with all of my backed-up garbage, it finally overflowed.

AFTER SEVERAL YEARS in a steady role at LA PALESTRA, an upscale residential fitness organization with a number of locations in New York City, I began to lose my motivation. I made it almost 8 years, which for me, was long. I think I lasted that long because the CEO gave me lots of freedom. Nevertheless, I started acting out again rather than addressing my career unhappiness head-on and making positive change, and I went back to my old ways. Only this time, I brought the self-destructive behavior to work. It was as if I wanted to be caught so that it would end. I could have ended it the right way and used it as a platform for growth.

I was working at one of the club's satellite locations, on the 30th floor in Times Square. With little supervision, I was charged with running the entire facility. I went to the only thing that I knew to quiet the unhappiness; I started bringing women into the gym during the workday, retiring to the massage room or my office, just steps away from members and staff who were traversing the main workout floor. There were many, many occasions wherein I was just seconds from being caught in flagrante delicto by one of the staff or a visit from a member. This went on for months. After seeing women come and go without checking in, everyone had started to have suspicions, especially the front desk staff, but I didn't care. These daily dalliances weren't helping me, but they would quiet my mind for a bit. But then the CEO started hearing rumors of my sexual shenanigans, and the staff submitted written accounts of these indiscretions.

The CEO summoned me into his office in early February 2014. I walked through the door feeling indifferent and rudderless, hoping he would just fire me right then and there. "Craig, what's been going on? I've got the staff telling me things I can't begin to believe," he said, putting me on the spot. "I don't know what they're all talking about," I replied, unfazed. My passive annoyance convinced him, as he dismissed me after only a few minutes of back and forth questioning. Two days later, I walk back into his office. "I'm resigning," I said as I handed him my written resignation letter. I quickly turned and walked out of the office. I blame myself, and only myself, for leaving unceremoniously. This last event really scared me, and I knew I needed change, but didn't know how. I left the home Grace and I shared and wandered the streets. Staying in random motels, continuing to indulge in God-awful and careless behavior, I was trying to find a way out, a way to end the failure and the turmoil I had caused. I didn't want to face Grace, to disappoint her, to hurt her. I loved her with all of my heart, and I had failed her.

After that terrible night that Grace rescued me from my misery on the street, she and I discussed the best course of action to get help me continue the road back. I called up an acquaintance who owned and operated an in-patient rehab facility for substance abuse. Though alcohol and drugs were not an issue for me, I was extremely self-destructive, and I was getting worse. Devoid of any compassion, I wasn't able to communicate without hurting people or turning them against me; my words were lined with spikes as they flowed through my lips. Grace bore the brunt of my attacks as I looked for ways to escape. I wanted to run away from the pain and deprecating thoughts that had left no occupancy for happiness or hope. Nothing seemed right. My behavior was unacceptable, even for myself. I was in reckless abandonment mode, full depression, with no off switch in sight.

Once the decision was made, I checked into rehab on a Friday in October and stayed for an 18-day program. As I walked into the facility, I turned and said goodbye to Grace. I had no doubt she would be there, smiling with warmth in her face, when my time there was complete.

As I walked through the automatic sliding front doors, I glanced back quickly at Grace, who still looked hopeful, and was softly smiling back at me. I passed a security guard, dressed in his tan uniform; he followed me with his eyes as I walked up to the front desk, off to the right.

The receptionist checked me in and walked me to the back. "Craig, come on back with me so we can get you checked in." the large brunette said to me as she got up from her desk.

I was processed. They asked me to strip down, and they did a full body search and scan, took my possessions, and gave me an orange jumper. "Put this on, please, and we will get you your clothing back later today."

The walls were white, sterile, with a hint of warmth coming from the staff, the minimalist décor, and the subtle additions of color throughout the hallway floor tiles. There was a wide range of people there, some young and some older. Some of these individuals were abusers, allowing their vice to make them physically harm those in their lives. Some younger residents seemed happy, maybe in need of more attention than they could get at home. It was the perfect place for those young adults. There was no void of attention here. Staff and residents alike were lining the halls and meeting rooms constantly. I remember thinking about how many emotions were now 'locked' into the same facility.

They held meetings to 'talk' things out. I had no compassion for anyone around me for the first few days. I was tired, irritable, and in an environment that made me uncomfortable. My desired solidarity was being ripped away, of my own account. Roaming the hallways with wrist bands and staff, I knew all the dirty little secrets of every resident. To be in the patients' heads, what a treasure trove of stories they must have had! The staff was working amongst a Pandora's box of offenders, addicts, and self-destructive people.

I tried to assimilate, but I still preferred to spend time alone. You basically stay there as long as your insurance will pay, so each person's program length is different. For me, it was helpful. I was given the opportunity to pull over and step outside myself. As one speaker said while I was there, "It doesn't matter what you are indulging in. If it hurts you, it's gotta go."

I would walk around the building every day, all day, when I wasn't in a scheduled class. Thinking and thinking, I was reliving my experiences and looking at the road ahead. I imagined what would be next in my career and for Grace and me. I knew I needed to step up. During the next few weeks, I got on board. I tried to listen in the meetings. I tried to pull out the nuggets that would help me get on the right trajectory. This was my chance to embrace help, slow down, and learn. On the night before I was scheduled to leave, I was asked to tell 'my story' to the entire inpatient community and staff. This was the first time I had ever said any of this out loud or shared my experiences with anyone. I owned the craziness of my mother's love affairs and personal ads, having witnessed her sexual escapades and trying to recreate those scenes with my first high school girlfriend. I spoke about the scandalous nights of high-risk sex-for-hire partners, hours spent prepping and canvasing these women, and giving the 'yes' or 'no' signal for them to enter. I went through how I always ended up with the wrong crowd; men, whom I would grow to admire, while all they did was impart more self-doubt and volatility into my days, and wreck my overall self-esteem. I recounted how I met Grace; I told how even in her strength I had continued to fall. I wrapped up by finally admitting that I had never indeed known myself and how the cycle of destruction kept repeating; disaster would happen, and then I would flee the scene, running as fast as I could. I admitted this was the first time, standing there in front of them, that I wanted to take account for my actions, for the love that was made so selflessly from Grace, and that it deserved my attention and respect.

During that speech, I realized I could stand up for more than I had ever given myself credit for in the past. It was very freeing, and I made a promise to myself that I would always own my experiences and not edit for anyone, or anything.

I finished the program, whatever that means, and was discharged in the morning after day 18. Grace was, indeed, waiting outside for me with a smile on her face. We hopped in the car and headed over to Valley Forge Military Academy, which was nearby. It was a beautiful fall day, and I was hopeful that good things lay ahead.

We walked around the public areas of the campus as I recalled being here during my years as a cadet. It was a healthy experience to see the campus and to breath in some fresh, non-city air. We took in the scenery and reveled in its serenity. For a moment, nothing else seemed to matter. Walking with Grace, pausing and thinking about her and my responsibility to my commitment, was one of the first moments I felt like the man I had been chasing to become. No titles were needed, just accountability and action to my wife and myself.

Though my brothers and sister were informed of my rehab visit, they never reached out. I guess it was because all of them were dealing with different problems in their own lives. Issued with kids, divorce, and being reclusive in their actions were all a gross byproduct of our upbringing. It was a time of vulnerability unknown to me. I now knew that Grace was my family, and I owed her more than I had shown up to this point.

After rehab, it was time to move on. This time it was going to be intentional. No running away, as I would be running toward something instead. With Grace by my side, we started looking for an opportunity to acquire a business. After only a few short weeks of searching, there was an opportunity to acquire a yoga studio in Westchester, New York. The combination of Grace, who was now a certified yoga instructor, and me with my background in fitness, seemed like a smart and calculated move. It would be a fresh start, pursuing the thing that had brought us together so many years before, and this time I really wanted to do it right.

Bikram yoga completely changed my life in many ways. Not only did it bring Grace and me together, but it also changed my view and approach to fitness. And it helped me manage my emotions. Buying the studio was an enormous investment with so many of our assets on the line. Grace and I sold our apartment and used the money from the sale to make a cash offer. Something was exhilarating about the entire process. We both felt that new beginnings were in store for us. After a few twists and turns during the negotiations and a full diagnostic of the business we took ownership. We took possession of the keys after successfully leaving the closing, and it was a day of extreme fulfillment for Grace and me. We were excited to have found something we could conquer together, be a team, and work on to help each other.

Right away, I began to renovate and change operations. I analyzed every aspect of the business, from the aesthetics, physical infrastructure, operations, sales, and programs. I started making necessary changes to the programming. By making some solid and smart upgrades, I brought in a more diverse fitness matrix and membership program. Part of this included offering more services to entice new members and bringing in a diversified staff to create new energy in the facility. I saw financial sustainability as a big issue and added EFT (electronic debit) to the purchase agreements. Business doubled almost overnight through being able to collect payments, offering comprehensive membership packages, and, most of all, providing value.

I enjoyed the process, and it was great not having to collaborate and be a part of a team. I realized how much I really lacked in that department! I have always struggled to consistently communicate in a polite and cordial manner or understood the boundaries of political correctness. In short bursts, I did great, but full days of actually talking to staff were like nails on a chalkboard to me.

We operated the studio for over a year. Our mission was to make it profitable, attract buyers, and then sell it. I had no idea how much I had absorbed from all the fitness mentors I had, but it was like having a highlight reel ready and on-call during the whole process. If I hadn't recognized the deficits in the facility before buying, and made strategic, high-impact renovations, and key changes to the matrix, we would not have done the studio justice and missed the opportunity to attract big buyers.

This environment, in particular, was challenging. Grace especially didn't like the business aspect. I guess there is this idea that owning a yoga studio is a chill and easy lifestyle, but at the end of the day, it's still a business. At this time, we were seeing a decline in interest due to the highly publicized sexual misconduct and rape allegations levied against Bikram Choudhury, the pioneer of the hot yoga movement. We changed the name of the studio to rebrand, and to a degree, it worked. We attracted a hefty price tag for the studio, and after the sale, the new business owners hired me on as a consultant to leverage my expertise through the transition of ownership. I did enjoy this, as long as they listened to my direction. While I liked driving change and being respected as a thought leader in the industry, I was anxious to make a clean separation and move on. To solidify my exit from the studio, I started applying to local gyms for director-level roles in personal training.

I landed a role and began a very short stint as Director of Personal Training for Blink Fitness in New York City. I quickly realized how little patience I had with anyone who didn't see my vision, and I clashed quickly with the VP of Operations. I woke up one day and decided enough was enough. "Joe, I am no longer motivated to be in this role and am tired of being micromanaged," I started my email to my supervisor. After another two paragraphs wherein I likened him to the character 'Kramer' from the show "Seinfeld", I pointed out how I felt he constantly inserted himself into everyone's business with little or no positive contribution or understanding. Thus, he made things worse and forced everyone else to clean up after him. When I wrote my email, I couldn't imagine that I could have ever come back from that. I guess that's why I said it! I quickly pressed send before I redacted any of my harsh words. In retrospect, it wasn't one of my finer professional decisions.

SESSION 13: PHILADELPHIA FREEDOM

To build company morale before the grand opening of a new club in Center City, we organize a one-day retreat. It isn't 'we'; it's the others on the executive team. I'm supposed to be coordinating the event and acting as the official emcee, but instead, the other VP's conspire together and take over my responsibilities, and I'm relegated to being by myself. I am no longer a part of the 'cool clique'. Instead of sitting with them, I am circling the room. I no longer want to associate with the executive team. The feeling of being some imposter quickly creeps through my body.

This should be a clear sign to me that I am on the outs, but I'm really not interested in knowing more or being included. It's why I fail in the role, and I don't care.

Ironically, we rent a comedy club for the event. It is a very large, dimly-lit showroom with a huge platform stage. Even though it is 10 AM and the sun is shining outside, you'd never know it once you come further into the club. In the low lighting, one of the members of the executive team starts setting up the projector. All of us have prepared a PowerPoint presentation pertaining to our specific department, and we are all pulling out our notes.

"Hello, and welcome to our company retreat," the head of human

resources says. Boring, rote, and uninspiring, her talk does not elicit even a peep or mere clap from the crowd. A sleepy cloud lingers over the staff as she concludes.

After two more speakers, it's my turn. I leap up onto the side of the stage, after hearing my intro, shifting the mood quickly and adding a new dynamic to the room. It takes everyone by surprise. And then, as soon as I feel the microphone in my hand, I have an incredible electric current of confidence. "Uh oh, it's coming out now, there's no turning back," I think to myself.

As soon as I grab the mic, I am in front of 200 uninspired and low-energy employees who have no idea where I am going with this. Everyone can tell something different going on. Some are staring in horror, others are looking on in pleasant surprise, and each is sitting an inch higher in their seats. I think they are saying to themselves, "This guy is totally going off the rails, and I love it!"

I don't realize until I am onstage that I have retained much of my previous stand-up routine material. Of course, I add a few improvised observations about my experiences with the company over the last several months. Without thinking about it, I completely abandon my slides and go on to perform 20 minutes of stand-up material.

And it all comes full circle for me. I keep looking at the audience in that dark club, and I don't see the executive team or the employees. In my head, I am playing to a crowd of people on dates, people after work, people wanting to escape with some comedy. It's not a conscious decision. Words keep coming out of my mouth. Ten am feels like 10 pm on a Friday night, in a packed club, performing a comedy set.

It is utter confusion. I have a moment of clarity, realizing that I'm holding the room's attention at this point. I then hear an audible laugh come from the executive team's table after one joke.

In contrast to this executive position, it is in the comedy clubs where I feel alive. At this moment in the comedy club, all professionalism, everything that isn't authentically Craig Maltese, leaves my body. A power comes over me. All that exists is storytelling and my true self.

"You know, in this role, I made many mistakes. Hey, if you don't believe me, ask Kent!" I talk to the audience while pointing to Kent, the

CEO, who is also my boss. I am determined to flip every stone in front of the entire company. And I know I can never put these stones back in place again. It is absolute freedom.

All of the executive team are supposed to share headshots or pictures of ourselves on the screen.

"I would share my picture, but I'm still wanted in a few states," I say, and point to Richard, the corporate lawyer. People are flabbergasted, laughing, and now interested.

When I walk off the stage, I walk right in front of Kent. He says, "Hey Craig, that was funny. You should be on stage. I have some connections."

Aha, I think to myself. The lightbulb clicks on. He is polite to me the same way they had been when I was in high school, and they wanted to get rid of me. He doesn't feel the need to correct me because he knows I am already out the door. And he knows I want to be out the door. And I have just made a choice for him.

And as expected, a week later, Kent lets me go from my position. His parting words are, "There are probably better things out there for you, Craig." Do you know what that is? It's what you say when it is awkward, and you don't know what to say to someone. I know he is just saying that to mask his own disappointment and frustration with me, but I know he is right. I just don't own it...YET.

I STAYED out of the fitness scene for a couple of years and took some much-needed time off to plan my next move. After years of winging it, I hired a career coach, revamped my resume, and did a full rebrand of myself. "What is your target, Craig?" my career coach asked. "I want to be at that executive level. I have all of the experience and have never had the title. I want to position myself for that level." With this new image, I landed a role as Vice President of Operations for a mid-sized fitness company in Philadelphia.

I was pumped. I remember recounting the interview process to my coach and how excited I felt. "They were straight with me, they need my talents, and I know I can make some major differences to their operations," I exclaimed. The reality, though, would hit me like a ton of bricks. I toured all of the facilities to get acquainted. The millennials behind the desk were looking at me like I was from another planet and time period. As the days passed, I began to question myself and my sanity.

After my first quarter, I was called into the office by the CEO. "Craig, I don't know where to start. I've collected feedback from the staff at different facilities and need to share their words with you." "Their words?" I thought to myself, "what words?" I sat in disbelief in the next lines. "Craig, you are brash and hurtful in your approach. Many team members feel that you are not encouraging and have too many expectations that they cannot meet. Additionally, your peers find you moody and unpredictable in their dealings with you. I need you to think about your approach and what you can change to help them feel more comfortable with you," he relayed.

My ego was enraged! I called my career coach and spewed. "What the hell do they want me to do? Coddle the staff, tell them it's okay that they aren't actually doing their job?" I said heatedly. "Are you able to have weekly meetings with your staff to allow them to speak up and share wins and difficulties?" she asked. "No, I'm not doing any of that," I replied quickly. "Can you?" she asked, genuinely not sure of my answer. As much as I hated it, I agreed to try. The fix actually worked for a couple of weeks until I realized, I loved the IDEA of this job and this VP role but wanted NOTHING to do with actually executing it. I knew I had the experience and skill set to do the job, but doing it was a whole other thing. The company was assembling an executive team to transition into a corporate operational structure. I allowed ego to lead me here and quickly came to the realization that I just wanted the title, but no longer had the desire or willingness to collaborate and be a part of a team, or any team, for that matter.

During the month-long interview process, and early on after beginning the role, I can vividly remember liking the company's

CEO, Kent, my prospective boss. He shared his story and his early struggles from his experiences in the fitness industry. His vision for the future resonated with me. Initially, I found Kent's story compelling, but as time passed, I became disengaged. The Kool-Aid I initially had allowed to fuel me was no longer appealing to my taste buds. My distaste quickly turned to resentment. I could no longer buy into the brand or to the CEO's story or mission.

I didn't want to work that hard in this last role. I just thought I could initiate strategies and programs, but I didn't want to mix it up with people. I was ready to be the delegator, not the doer. Interacting with people daily was more exhausting for me than ever. Every generation has its faults, but I found millennials generally to be extra annoying, entitled, and lacking in charisma, toughness, raw talent, and personality. I know that is not a new observation, but that has been my experience working with them.

Let me be clear, as I have spent a lot of time trying to say this nicely and transparently. I don't dislike people, and I am not misanthropic, but I do not enjoy being around people in traditional settings. I hate parties in all their forms, including meetings, conference calls, luncheons, and socializing as we know it. I hated greeting everyone every single day in a highly happy fashion, feeling the obligation to play a character in a child's play. I was in a role for which I had to adopt this persona, and it was unpleasant, draining, and joyless. After constant bouts of mindless chatter and mini self-esteem workshops, I hated it and dreaded walking into each gym. It was so bad that I felt nauseous each time! I realize how fortunate I had been in my career to have been given a lot of freedom in my previous roles. Some were by design, and others were just symptomatic of the culture.

This makes it difficult for me to exist in a community, let alone thrive and enjoy it. This last role was the toughest, and I had the least amount of patience and motivation to meet it. Kent wasn't evil. I felt he didn't take the time to meet me on any level but his own, and that allowed my influence across the company to diminish. I had had enough. I was ready to let the shot clock run down to zero.

This role represented my last-ditch effort to make a name for myself, in the industry I had once loved, but now have come to despise.

To build company morale and improve culture, the executive team organized a one-day retreat. This was when I performed 20 minutes of stand-up material in the comedy club.

It was the best I had felt in years, as that material flowed out of me. I did say all of these things that were against the corporate culture. I knew with each word, I was closing the door on my fitness career, and I was fine with it. In fact, I was more than fine with it! I enjoyed being in front of a crowd rather than part of one interacting with people on the same platform.

Sometimes diplomacy needs to take a backseat to unilateral action. The arm's length distance from people was where I most enjoyed being and performing, not placating and pacifying, which was so much a part of my role. I felt so uncomfortable with following the executive team's lead that being myself with that mic, in front of the audience that day, felt like my true calling.

Within a week, my fitness career officially concluded. I am not an activist, nor am I vocal or passionate about many things. But I have come to question, and in many respects, detest the very industry I once loved, that I had spent over 2 decades. It wasn't always like this!

As a generation Xer, living in urban America, I can't help but wonder who I am, who I should be, and who I can become. This question has haunted me for years. I sometimes still get caught in the vortex and heaviness of the thought. I remember so vividly my last interactions with my mom, my dad, Bruce, John, Goose, and Phil. Each of these relationships had such a profound impact in my life. I still wonder who I am. I ask myself, "Am I a fitness guy, a businessman, a free spirit, or just a fraud?" I've never actually answered that throughout all of my roles in fitness. I ask now, am I an iconoclast or just dysfunctional?

The adversity I endured as a young man was pivotal to my spiraling throughout my life. My years of sexual grifting, craving significance, and avoiding and running away from responsibility, were caused because I had no idea what love was, what it meant, or how it could feel. Love was a naughty word, and 'slut' was revered and powerful. My mother's sexual proclivity, the porn just waiting for me in the closet, and my inability to speak about feelings without judgement toward myself or others, left me scarred with baggage that I never actually saw until years later. As an adult and a husband, I recall those events and have tried to find humor in it all, knowing that through that lens, it just doesn't hurt as much.

Bruce currently resides in the Baltimore area where he owns and operates a very successful chain of franchised fitness centers across the Northeast. We have connected over the years, as I have run into him on a few occasions, and we've had several phone conversations. Our conversations are polite, cordial, and full of reminiscing about the old days; neither of us have ever brought up our falling out or the circumstances surrounding it. I am hopeful that one day we will embrace our past, not just the good, but the bad, and the ugly too, and reconcile fully with who we are today.

John and I never repaired our relationship, and it continues to weigh heavily inside me. I wish our relationship had come to a better end. We pretended we were people we really weren't, and therefore ours was never a sustainable friendship.

Goose was released from prison in the summer of 2019. We used to write to each other from time to time, and have recently started speaking again. We now both have wives we respect and care about. I'm working through the emotions of what contact with him brings to Grace and me. He spent over 20 years of his life locked away for his choices. He has since apologized for not being as good a friend as he could have been and putting my safety in jeopardy. He seems to be on track to finding peace with his actions and starting his life anew.

I took a trip in 2018 back to California and visited Phil. It was as though no time had passed, even though it had been 20 years. We spent our time together the way we always had, talking about life, and sharing our honest thoughts. We just enjoyed the laughter and chemistry between us that no amount of distance, space or time can diminish. His body is almost entirely covered with tattoos now. I felt he was hiding behind the safety of his tattoos, that each one held a deeper meaning, a secret memory, that was easier to express through art on his body than actually dealing with it. He married for a second time, had another child, and is still training clients as an independent trainer. I left our meeting knowing full well that he is still searching for the bigger, better life out there.

My brothers and sister remain behind the scenes in my life. I love them. If they needed a kidney, I'd be there, and I'd help them. However, we'd get separate rooms during recovery. I last saw my eldest brother, Tony, years ago. I remember, at the time in my 30's, when I woke up and saw his car gone the next morning, I cried, just as I did as a kid when he dropped us back at Mommy's. The emotions run high, and we have found some solace in embracing that as our reality.

My brother Dino resides in Nashville, remains married to his second wife, and has had a second chance at fatherhood with two young children. He put himself through college working two and three jobs at times and worked his way to place of wisdom, peace and prosperity. I was very slow to develop a sense of self and responsibility which still remains a challenge for me at times. That remains a point of contention between Dino and me, though we rarely speak of it. He was there for Grace when I wasn't, offering her support and insights into the self-destructive behaviors that he has seen so many times before in the brother he tried so hard to set straight. He made things work, I made excuses; he took responsibility, and I squandered opportunities. It will take a lifetime to earn his respect, trust and love...I don't know if we will ever fully get there, and that's all on me.

As children, my sister Claudine and I were very close. I am so glad that she did not inherit any of my bad habits and self-destructive behaviors, as she was exposed to much of it during our childhood and early adulthood. She has also remarried, with two young children, and resides in an affluent enclave in Orange County, California. And just like our mother, she has taste for the good life, and has found it. She is a constant reminder to me of our mother, a mirror image in every sense, which is a large part of the reason why I shy away from interaction with her. Just hearing her voice sends an unpleasant surge of energy up my spine. I love her; I just can't be around her. We rarely communicate and haven't seen each other in years, but our past is real and it lives in me.

I've spent a lot of my life not knowing how to channel my parents; their personalities and actions were both helpful and harmful. Somewhere in the middle is where I'd like to rest. Later in life, Dino said to me, "Take the best from each of them and let the rest go."

My dad was incredibly kind, generous, and a great listener, though he seldom followed anyone's words or advice, even when it was in his best interest. He was a chronic procrastinator, extremely introverted at times, but never stopped trying to improve the quality of his life. He just ran out of time!

I've found an avenue to offer people a piece of my pain through a channel of prospective growth. Does this mean I'm ready to make more friends and be a socialite? Nope. Not even close. No amount of healing will get me to change my comfort in solidarity, my quip, and attitude toward group hugs. I still have no tolerance toward someone's unilateral wet dream when I know that won't ever be successful. Nope.

I'm fortunate to be here, to be writing this, and have the liberty to share it. The next step is to avoid fitness like the plague and perceive it as the monastery, taking all pleasure of it from my life. Whatever the visual, the metaphor I need to tell myself is that I will finally be pursuing my future, one of growth, one of happiness, and one of living my truth.

Grace was, and still is the only person who truly believes in me. She knew I could be much more than what I thought of myself. She always said to me, "I am your wife, that's what I do," but she went far beyond that, and she is the only person who really knows me!

There is absolutely no way I would be alive today without her.

She has been a source of comfort, safety, fun, and fulfillment in my life that I never expected to feel. Without her influence, I would have continued to self-sabotage to the point of no return. No matter what I do in my life, whatever my accomplishments might be, the best thing I have ever done is marry Grace. She is the best part of every day for me.

I still experience what I call the 'witching hours'. These are certain times of the day where I feel uncomfortable from the shadow in which I grew up. When I lived with my mom and Bernie, the instability and the negative feelings generated made me dread certain days and certain times of the day. Saturday afternoons still feel weird to me, as that was when I had my worst and most memorable moments with Bernie. And I often returned from weekends with my dad to my mom's house on Sundays, so I have been branded with feelings of fear and misery on those days. It's better than it used to be, but it is still there.

For me, it is time to take the stage. Sometimes you just can't hide your truth, and I couldn't any longer. I had to get back to being on stage performing, wherever it took me. It's the one place I never felt I had to hide my raw thoughts and always felt alive. The stories I've compiled throughout my life no longer have a purpose of being littered by guilt but instead belong out in the world, bringing people new perspectives. I'm ready to get out there, expose my story, and share the humor that has been my guiding light with the rest of those who want to be a part of it. For me, it is time to sit down to STAND UP!

I can finally say to the memory of my father, "I am somebody. I am doing something with myself and embracing it." It's taken decades to come to this realization, and I plan to enjoy it for decades more. I am finally living in the light, not comparing myself to the shadows left by those in my family. Now I am engaging only in the things that bring me success on my terms. No more working for people who talk but don't take action, and those who pander to the whims of every employee, but avoid adversity. I'm done. I officially resign from the world of fitness, which is becoming ever more corporate and image-based. It's more about marketing, more about style and the realization that the fitness industry business model is based on the member giving up on themselves and giving in to their terms.

I've spent most of my life according to a clock, from one measurement to another, from hour to hour 'sessions' to monthly to quarterly to yearly as I climbed the corporate ladder of the fitness industry. I enjoy the freedom that comes without the obligations of meetings, phone calls, reports, emails, and on and on. Now I enjoy communication in its rawest and most irregular forms, which has no place in the professional business world. I've embraced my weaknesses, and I find humor and comfort in them.

My life is now about addressing these sessions and the other moments of my life. I plan to spend the rest of my life on stage, revisiting these moments over and over.

REFERENCES

Preface - Goodreads.com, Christopher Hitchens Quotes; https://www.goodreads.com/quotes/35925-everybody-does-have-a-book-in-them-but-in-most

Session 1 - *Forest Gump.* Directed by Robert Zemeckis. Hollywood, CA: Paramount Pictures, 1994.

Tinder is the trademark of Match Group, LLC.

Pontiac Grand Prix is the trademark of the Pontiac Division of General Motors.

Dallas (TV Series) Created by David Jacobs. Produced by Lorimar Productions. (1978-1991).

The Sopranos (TV Series) Created by David Chase. Produced by Chase Films, Brad Grey Television, and HBO Entertainment. (1999-2007).

"Playboy" magazine is a trademark of Playboy Enterprises, Incorporated.

"Penthouse" magazine is a trademark of Penthouse Global Media and General Media Communications.

Rocky II. Directed by Sylvester Stallone. Hollywood, CA: United Artists, 1979.

Session 2 - *The Lawrence Welk Show* (TV Series) Presented by

Lawrence Welk. Produced by Teleklew Productions (1955–1982), American Broadcasting Company (1955–1971). Distributed by Don Fedderson Productions (1971–1982) (1951–1955, 1955-1971, in syndication 1971-1982).

Session 5 - Gold's Gym is the trademark of Gold's Gym.

YMCA is the trademark of YMCA of the USA.

Session 6 - Perfetto™ is the trademark of Hiltl Holding GmbH /HILTL PERFETTO trademark.

General Hospital (TV Series) Created by Frank and Doris Hursley. Produced by Selmur Productions (1963–1968), <u>ABC</u> (1968–present). Distributed by <u>American Broadcasting Company</u>. (1963-).

Bandaids are a trademark of Johnson & Johnson Corporation.

Beningan's is the trademark of Legendary Restaurant Brands, LLC.

Camaro is the trademark of <u>General Motors.</u>

Session 7 - Smith, Will. "Will Smith Gettin Jiggy Wit It (Official Version)" YouTube.

https://www.youtube.com/watch?v=3JcmQONgXJM

Session 8 - Gatorade is a trademark of <u>Stokely-Van Camp, Inc.</u>

Session 9 - Jägermeister is a trademark of Mast-Jaegermeister SE.

Koo-Koo-Roos is the trademark of Luby's Restaurants Incorporated.

Session 11 - Starbucks is the trademark of Starbucks Corporation.

Honda Civic is the trademark of Honda Motor Company, Ltd.

Session 12 - LA PALESTRA is the trademark of LA PALESTRA Incorporated.

Blink Fitness is a trademark of Blink Holding Inc.

Seinfeld (TV Series) Created by Larry David and Jerry Seinfeld. Produced by West-Shapiro, Castle Rock Entertainment. (1989-1998).

Session 13 - Kool-Aid is the trademark of <u>Kraft Foods Group Brands LLC.</u>

ABOUT THE AUTHOR

As an accomplished business owner, managing director, and writer across the Fitness Industry, Craig Maltese has a unique insider's perspective, having worked with some of the industry's great leaders and innovative minds. He has worked in the trenches, having experience across every level of the business sector. He currently writes and contributes to fitness publications and podcasts and provides business consulting services to new business owners. Craig is a provocative, sharp-tongued professional who is open to humility and forges a path far from the flock. He garners the talent for provoking laughter from inside even the tightest corners of one's impervious mouth. Recounting his childhood and understanding how much impact it really had on his path, his failures, and ultimately his successes is something that he has learned to do through humor. He undergoes a constant battle against who he was programmed to be during those critical development years and who he truly wants to be and become.

Facebook.com/craigmaltesesessions
Twitter.com/MalteseCraig
LinkedIn.com/CraigMaltese
craig.maltese13@gmail.com